FAMOUS MISSIONARIES

Famous Missionaries of The Reformed Church

BY

REV. JAMES I. GOOD, D.D.

Professor of Dogmatics and Reformed Church History in the Ursinus School of Theology

Author of "Women of the Reformed Church," "Historical Manual of the Reformed Church," "History of the Reformed Church in the United States," "History of the Reformed Church of Germany," Etc.

SOLID GROUND CHRISTIAN BOOKS
BIRMINGHAM, ALABAMA USA

Solid Ground Christian Books
PO Box 660132
Vestavia Hills AL 35266
205-443-0311
sgcb@charter.net
solid-ground-books.com

Famous Missionaries of the Reformed Church
by James I. Good (1850-1924)

First published in 1903 by The Sunday-School Board of the Reformed Church in the United States
First Solid Ground edition October 2009

Cover image is Francis Coillard (see p. 111).
Cover design by Borgo Design, Tuscaloosa, AL

ISBN: 978-159925-225-4

INTRODUCTION.

THE gulf stream of modern Christianity is Christian missions. On and on, while the chilling winds from the desolate shores of doubt vex and rock the whole sea of Christian truth, this influence keeps steadily flowing towards the frozen zones of heathenism. Already these Arctic shores of desolation and chill begin to shoot forth such verdure as grows upon the banks of the River of Life.

Because of the recent revival of missionary activity in the Reformed Church we are in danger of forgetting that this candle never went out. There were times when it was burning low, but it was burning. Though its shining was in one of the lower windows of the temple, yet its light was none the less steady; and the highway along which it shone was so bright that no man needed to stumble therein if he were searching for the Light of Life.

We rejoice then that such a successful effort has

been made to gather together in compact form the lives and doings of the missionaries, who in those days of difficult beginnings delighted to wage the warfare for the conquest of the world, under the Reformed banner. The reading of this volume will doubtless be a surprise to many. There are, we venture to assert, but very few who knew that we had such a respectable number of men and women who will be numbered among the heroic missionaries of the Church. It will be a revelation to very many who should have known better. We shall wonder that some former historian did not glean in such a rich field. But it may possibly have been reserved for such a time as this, when the missionary tide is swelling with such confidence, and which will need just such facts to steady it from feeling an ebb that might prove disastrous and disheartening. Guided by the experience and success of these consecrated missionaries, we will feel ourselves safer in casting into the treasury of the Lord the greater gifts that will be needed; and in consecrating our sons and daughters to this particular form of Christian work. Though there are other branches of the Church of Christ that have had a larger army in the field, yet taking all the circumstances we need not be ashamed of what we have done, and at what we are doing now. The experiences of the past will guide us in the future. Our sails are being set with a purpose of doing our share in the work of giving the Gospel to those who have long stretched out their hands in vain. We are catching the influence of that morning light which is breaking, and we are going up because we feel that the Lord is with us.

We rejoice that this book adds another to the growing literature of the Reformed Church. It is the very highest type of literature for an age that is being twisted and is not always sure of its bearings. From the consecration and devotion of the missionaries come the assurance that the Word and Spirit have not lost their power. These missionaries have gone forth in the power of the Spirit, and they have not preached and labored in vain. They have not been ashamed of the Gospel, and it has proved to be the power and wisdom of God unto the salvation of men. Some one asked a little while ago in a company of ministers what kind of literature should be placed into the hands of a young man who was disposed to be doubting. A hymn book, said one; a service book, said another; a life of Christ, said a third, like the Christ of History by John Young. We believe that nothing can be provided that will bring the doubter out of the unfortunate condition into which he has fallen than a faithful presentation of the triumphs and sacrifices of missionaries. Here is the apology that can not be answered. It presents facts that throb with flesh and blood. It is a heart to heart talk with one who can not help but realize that there is still power with God to raise up men and women who can give the Gospel to those who have not heard it, and move them to renounce the world and the flesh and the devil. A careful reading of this book will confirm the faith of those who are not affected by doubts and fears, and will lead the wandering spirit of the doubter to the fountain of everlasting life and healing.

CONRAD CLEVER.

Baltimore, Md.

INDEX.

	PAGE
INTRODUCTION.	

BOOK I. EARLY REFORMED MISSIONS.

CHAPTER I.

The First Reformed Missionaries to Brazil......... 7

CHAPTER II.

The Dutch Reformed Seminary under Walaeus at Leyden 21

CHAPTER III.

The Dutch Reformed Missionaries in Brazil........ 33

CHAPTER IV.

The Dutch Reformed Mission in Formosa—the Crucifixion of the Reformed...................... 37

BOOK II. THE REFORMED IN AFRICA.

CHAPTER I.

Theodosius Vanderkemp 51

CHAPTER II.

Eugene Casalis 71

CHAPTER III.

Adolphe Mabille.................................. 94

CHAPTER IV.
Francis and Christian Coillard.................... 110

CHAPTER V.
Paul Berthoud and Ernest Creux................. 135

CHAPTER VI.
Escande and Minault—the Reformed Martyrs...... 147

Book III. The Reformed in Asia.

A.—India.

CHAPTER I.
Alphonse F. Lacroix............................ 157

CHAPTER II.
John Scudder.................................... 189

CHAPTER III.
Jacob Chamberlain.............................. 205

B.—China.

CHAPTER IV.
David Abeel..................................... 222

CHAPTER V.
John Van Nest Talmadge........................ 235

CHAPTER VI.
William E. Hoy and the New Mission of the Reformed Church in the United States........... 245

C.—Japan.

Chapter VII.

Guido F. Verbeck 249

Chapter VIII.

The Mission of the Reformed Church in the United States 262

D.—Mohammedan Lands.

Chapter IX.

Benjamin C. Schneider 275

Chapter X.

Samuel M. Zwemer 289

Book IV. The Reformed in the East Indies.

Chapter I.

Jan Kam, the Apostle to the Moluccas 301

Chapter II.

Emde, the Watchmaker of Surabaya 317

Chapter III.

John F. Riedel 335

Book V. The Reformed in America.

Chapter I.

John Megapolensis 357

CHAPTER II.
George M. Weiss.. 367

CHAPTER III.
The Mission to the Winnebagoes.................... 373

CHAPTER IV.
The Indian Mission in Oklahoma................... 377

BOOK VI. THE REFORMED AMONG THE JEWS.

CHAPTER I.
The Wonderful Mission at Buda-Pesth............. 383

CHAPTER II.
Ferdinand W. Becker.............................. 399

Illustrations

Dr. Robert Junius	Opposite page 37
Dr. Theodosius Vanderkemp	Opposite page 51
Francis Coillard	Opposite page 111
Madame Christina Coillard	Opposite page 119
Rev. Benjamin Escande	Opposite page 150
David Abeel	Opposite page 223
Rev. Dr. Guido Verbeck in 1897	Opposite page 249
Rev. Dr. Benjamin Schneider	Opposite page 275

BOOK I.

Great Missionaries of the Reformed Church

EARLY REFORMED MISSIONS

IN the great work of saving the world, the Reformed Church has had an honorable part and it ought to be inspiration to our German Reformed to learn what has already been done. The name Reformed is larger than any one nation or denomination. By famous missionaries of the Reformed Church we mean missionaries who under the Reformed name have gone forth and preached the gospel to the heathen. For the Reformed, whether Dutch, German, French, Swiss or American, are after all the same. The glory of one is the glory of all. Accordingly this subject is one of great interest to all our people. The Reformed missionaries have made the Reformed name known all over the world.*

---

*We have included in the list of missionaries some who were not particularly Reformed in their confessional learnings, but who were Reformed by birth or by association with some Reformed missionary society. The Reformed Church should have credit for these latter, in some way, as well as for the former.

Chapter I.

THE FIRST REFORMED MISSIONARIES TO BRAZIL.

The first Protestant missionaries were missionaries of the Reformed Church. Protestantism was hardly born before it began to exert itself to save the heathen. These missionaries were sent out one year before the Lutherans sent their first foreign missionaries to Lapland.

The first missionary field was this new world of America. To this continent came two ministers of the Reformed Church of Geneva whose names deserve to be embalmed in fame. They were Peter Richer and William Chartier. Admiral Coligny, the great statesman of the French Reformed, fearing the persecutions which afterward overtook the Huguenots, with far-seeing eye looked westward for an asylum across the Atlantic. Brazil was at that time attracting notice and through his influence a colony was gathered. But though this expedition was announced with a flourish of trumpets, it was found that too few were ready to go; so the jails of Paris were called upon to complete the company. This motley company, some of them Huguenots, sailed from Havre in the summer of 1555. After a long voyage they entered the bay of Rio Janeiro on the tenth of November. The leader of this expedition was Villegagnon. He had been Vice-Admiral of Brittany and the one who in 1548 had brought Mary, Queen of Scots, safely to France in spite of the watchfulness of the English. He had become a Protestant and now dreamt of founding a great French colony in the new world. Villegagnon selected an island in the bay of Rio Janeiro as his headquarters. On a rock near the centre of the island he built a rude home with a rough church on the one side of it, and a rude building for his followers on the other. He fortified the island with earthworks as he feared the Portuguese who already had planted colonies in Brazil. He named the island Coligny, and the whole region Antarctic France.

On the fourth of February one of his ships sailed for France. With it he sent a messenger to Coligny asking for more colonists and especially for Reformed ministers who should not only minister to the colonists but also plant this new faith among the Indians of the new world. Two ministers, Peter

The Reformed Church. 9

Richer and William Chartier, were appointed by the city of Geneva to go to Brazil. They were accompanied by eleven artisans from Geneva who were led by DuPont. They visited Coligny on their way through France where they were joined by a number of Huguenots. This new expedition, numbering 300, embarked November 17, 1556, in three ships from Honfleur. After being almost shipwrecked off the coast of Brazil they finally arrived at Rio Janeiro March 7, 1557. As they entered the harbor they were full of joy at the thought of planting the Reformed faith on so distant a coast. First of all Protestants they were to feel the peculiar joy that comes when telling the story of Christ for the first time to the heathen.

Villegagnon welcomed them with a salute from the fort and with every demonstration of friendship. They went at once to the church where they held a thanksgiving service. They sang the fifth Psalm, after which Richer preached on the 26th Psalm. Villegagnon ordered that there should be a daily service with a sermon of not over an hour and also two sermons on Sunday. On the 21st of March the two ministers administered the communion after the Reformed mode. This was the first Protestant communion in America, a forerunner of many rich spiritual feasts of the thousands of Reformed in this western world in later centuries. These ministers soon tried to come into contact with the natives of Brazil so as to bring them to Christ. Richer wrote, a few weeks after his arrival in Brazil, that "they proposed winning the native heathen to Christ, but their barbarism, their cannibalism, their spiritual dullness extinguished all these hopes." Their ignorance of the native language also hindered their work, but the natives understood enough from their teachings to become greatly astonished at what they heard. Some of them promised to become worshipers of the true God, but the stay of these missionaries at Rio Janeiro was too short to produce permanent results.

For soon troubles began to arise in the colony which prepared for its ultimate destruction. Among the first colonists who came with Villegagnon was John Cointat, or Hector, a former student of the Catholic Sorbonne at Paris. He claimed that he had been promised episcopal jurisdiction over the colony. He, however, at the first communion answered the questions of the ministers; but he resented this examination and soon called Villegagnon's attention to certain rites in which he differed from these ministers. He also came into controversy with them on such doctrinal points as, "Is it lawful to mix water with wine at the Lord's Supper?" "May the sacramental bread be made of Indian corn?" etc. He requested that unleavened bread should be used at the communion, that baptism should be administered with salt and oil as well as with water, and that the officiating minister should wear vestments. The ministers stoutly withstood him. As Cointat had some learning and was of ready speech he soon interested Villegagnon so that when Richer preached against these customs Villegagnon became angry. At first he forbade Richer to preach, but afterwards permitted him, provided he would not speak on these subjects in dispute. However, he did not allow him to administer the sacraments. To heal the controversy it was proposed that these questions should be submitted to the Reformed Church of France for a decision and for that purpose Chartier sailed for France.

Meanwhile Villegagnon from being a protector of the Reformed was changing into their persecutor. No sooner had the vessel sailed than he declared he would submit the disputed points to no one but the

Catholic Sorbonne for a decision. The truth is that through the influence of the Cardinal of Lorraine, Villegagnon was being secretly won back to the Catholic Church. The Cardinal had written him a letter upbraiding him for leaving the Catholic faith. He became bolder and finally openly called Calvin the heretic. At last he demanded that Richer subscribe to the mass, the purgatory and other Romish doctrines. Richer refused. Villegagnon fearing an insurrection ordered DuPont and the Genevan party to leave the island in October 1557. He declared he would not have the Protestants on the island. But whither should they go? In all the new world there was not a Protestant colony save their own. They went across the bay to the mainland where they settled. Here the inhabitants kindly brought food to them and they returned the kindness by trying to teach them the Gospel.

It, however, soon became evident that they could not live there very long; yet Villegagnon refused to permit them to return to the fort. A French vessel happened to come into the harbor and DuPont tried to arrange that they should be taken back to France. The captain, however, refused to take them on board without Villegagnon's permission. This Villegagnon at first refused. But when DePont declared that they would go without it he reluctantly granted permission on one condition, namely, that they would take on board a closed chest. With a baseness seldom paralleled he placed in this chest a paper which contained certain charges against them. The chest was to be presented to the first judge in France, with whom they would come in contact; and this paper asked him to seize them as heretics and punish them with flames. Ignorant of this perfidy, they sailed on January 4, 1558, after a stay in Brazil of about ten months. They soon discovered that they had exchanged a wretched existence on land for a more wretched one on the sea. The vessel was slow and old. When she was out about seven days she sprang a leak. She seemed to be sinking so rapidly that it appeared as though nothing was before them but a grave in the ocean. Fortunately the sailors succeeded in stopping the principal leak, but the carpenter stated that the vessel was so old and worm-eaten as not to be fit for so long a voyage with so large a cargo. The captain being afraid that the crew would all leave him if he landed refused to turn back. He, however, offered a boat to any who wished to return to America then from ten to twenty leagues distant. He was more willing to do this as they were short of provisions.

Five of their number accepted this offer and went back to Brazil to be the first Protestants to suffer for their faith in foreign lands. They floated for four days using their clothes for sails. A severe storm threw them on the sixth day on the shore at the foot of a great mountain. They then proceeded to Riviere des Vases where the natives kindly cared for them. After a four days' rest they travelled four days and arrived at Villegagnon's settlement. They begged him to receive them, notwithstanding their differences of faith. At first he received them kindly, but he soon became suspicious that they were spies sent by DuPont, who would later return and attack the settlement. He then ordered them to sign a Romish confession of faith within 12 hours. This they refused to do. They ordered Bortel, the older and best educated among them, to draw up a confession of faith in reply to it, which they signed. From this Villegagnon decided that they were heretics and then arrested Bortel, and when he refused to recant, he brutally struck him with his fist and ordered him to be hurled from a high rock on the island into the sea. Another, Vermiel, was led to the same rock,

The Reformed Church. 15

and when he refused to recant, he, too, was thrown over into the sea. Bourdon, the third, was sick in bed, but Villegagnon had him bound and carried in a boat to this rock of execution and from it cast into the sea. "Thus," says Kalkar, the Danish Lutheran historian of missions, "was the first blood shed as a witness for Evangelical missions." The Reformed Church as it had the honor of sending the first missionaries to the heathen, had also the honor of having the first martyrs for missions.

One of the five who returned from the ship was John Boles, a man of education and ability, about whom the Jesuit annals themselves revealed a strange tale. He was learned in both Hebrew and Greek. Having escaped from Villegagnon he went to St. Vincente, 300 miles southward (near the present Santos), where the Jesuits were laboring among the Indians. He preached to the Indians with such eloquence that there was danger of their becoming Protestants. The Jesuits became alarmed and being unable to answer his arguments, had him arrested together with several of his converts. He was taken to Bahia where he was imprisoned for eight years. When the Portuguese expelled the French from Bahia in 1567, the government had

Boles put to death on the site of the present Rio Janeiro. The Jesuits boasted that Anchieta, their great apostle in Brazil, won him back to Catholicism on the eve of his execution, and then showed them how to dispatch a heretic as quickly as possible by having him put to death. The story of his recantation is very doubtful, but evidently this colony of Villegagnon's left some such Protestant influence behind it in South America or the Jesuit records would not so strangely confess it.

In the meantime those who remained on the vessel, which these five had left, seemed doomed to a living death. A hundred times a day it seemed as if the ship would be swallowed up by the waves. The crew were kept at the pumps night and day and still were hardly able to keep the water down. One day as the carpenter was mending the ship a plank gave way. In a moment the sea came rushing in with the force of a torrent. The sailors rushed to the deck crying "We are lost." The carpenter, however, retained presence of mind enough to thrust his coat into the hole and by treading on it with all his might he resisted the force of the water. He soon received help which enabled him to keep the hole shut till he had prepared a board to close it. At another time when the powder was drying some of it caught fire. The flames quickly ran from one end of the ship to the other and set the sails and cordage on fire. Four men were burned before it was put out, one of them dying. Then to their horrors was added starvation. They had with them a number of parrots and monkeys which they were taking home as curiosities. These were soon eaten. Rats and mice were hunted for and eaten. Even the sweepings of the store-room were gathered and cooked into a sort of pottage and though it was black and bitter they were glad to eat it. Those who had bucklers made of the skin of the tapiroussa, an animal of Brazil, cut the skin into pieces and devoured it. Others would chew the covers of their trunks and the leather of their shoes—yes, even the horns of the ship lanterns. They became so starved that they would have been glad to have lived on grass, like Nebuchadnezzar, had they been able to get it. Finally nothing was left them but Brazil-wood, said to be the dryest of all woods. One day Peter Corquilleray when putting a piece of Brazil-wood into his mouth said to Lery (who wrote the chronicle of this journey) "Gladly would I give the four thousand louvres due me in France for a glass of wine and a pennyworth of bread." Peter Richer the Reformed minister was so prostrated by hunger that he could not lift up his head even in prayer, although he was almost constantly in prayer. Indeed, owing to the intensity of the sufferings it is wonderful that they did not select some one to be killed in order to satisfy the hunger of all.

Finally after a voyage of five months the pilot declared he saw land. This was very fortunate for the captain said that he had determined on the next day to draw lots that one might be killed for food. They finally landed on the coast of Brittany in France, near L'Orient, at the mouth of the Blavet river, on May 26, 1558. The inhabitants, touched with the story of their sufferings, kindly gave them the food and sustenance they needed. Many of the sailors, however, neglected the precautions necessary for starved men, and ate so heartily that they died. Others recovered but were afflicted for a long time with various diseases—blindness, swellings of the body, etc.

And now appeared the providence of God. In the sealed box was the order of Villegagnon to the governor of the province in which they landed to put them to death as heretics. The box was given by them, all ignorant of its contents, to the judge of that district; but by a favoring providence they were cast ashore in a part of France where the judge happened to be favorable to the Protestants. Instead of executing the treacherous orders of Villegagnon he ignored them and treated the returning colonists with great kindness. Soon after, in 1560, Villegagnon's colony in Brazil was captured by the Portuguese, when he returned to France where he tried to clear himself of his cruelty and perfidy which had now become known to all the world. A witness to the existence of the colony is still found in the harbor of Rio Janeiro in one of its islands which is named Villegagnon after him.*

Such were the first efforts to send missionaries to the heathen, but this early though ill-fated effort proved that the Reformed were the first who had the desire to send foreign missionaries and also the first to have been martyrs for their faith in foreign lands. They thus attempted to lay the basis of what

---

*Six years later Coligny tried a second colony under Ribaut who aimed to found a western asylum at Charles-fort, and Carolina in Florida, but this was soon destroyed by the Spaniards who then founded St. Augustine. No direct missionary work, however, was done among the natives. Still it is a very interesting bit of Reformed history in the new world. An interesting novel (based on Parkham's histories) entitled "St. Augustine," by Musick, describes this colony.

has become the greatest movement of the Protestant Church—foreign missions. The bay of Rio Janeiro is said to be the most beautiful in the world, but is not so beautiful as the crown of immortal glory that should belong to Richer and his co-laborers for starting a movement which has culminated in the splendid foreign missionary work of the Church at the present time.

Chapter II.

THE DUTCH REFORMED SEMINARY UNDER WALAEUS AT LEYDEN.

The Reformed, as they were the first to attempt the evangelization of the heathen, were also the first to found a Seminary for the training of missionaries to the heathen. In the seventeenth century the Reformed Church of the Netherlands was foremost in missions. In its day it equalled the British and American Missionary Societies together as they existed early in the nineteenth century, its aim being to open up missionary work both in the Eastern and Western hemispheres.

In 1596 the Dutch East India Company was organized for the purpose of carrying Dutch commerce to the East Indies. But they did not forget religion. Very early in its history chaplains to the Europeans were appointed, many of whom became missionaries among the heathen as well as chaplains.*

---

*The first minister ever ordained by the Protestants especially for its foreign missions was Casper Wiltens who went to Amboyna in 1615 laboring there till 1625. Even before him Philip Peterson had gone as the first chaplain to the East Indies in 1598 with the Dutch fleet. He went to Mauritius, preached Christ there, and baptized a slave of Madagascar. The first minister who was pastor of a congregation of converted Malays was Dubbeldryk, whose services in Malay were begun August 3, 1620.

But where were they to get ministers who would go into their far-away possessions? Who would brave the awful dangers of the seas from shipwreck and pirates and the equal dangers of the land from fever and savages? Feeling this want they asked the classes of Holland for advice. At first it seemed to them it would be sufficient were they to aid some young men to enter the ministry. In 1603 they determined to seek for two ministers to preach in India. In 1605 they determined to pay the expenses of four students, if they could be found, but no one applied until the next year. It was very evident that matters could not continue in that way or they would get no ministers for their colonies. Different plans were suggested to supply the need. In 1610 a few capable men, pupils of Prof. Walaeus, the professor of theology at Leyden, were approached but they were too few. Finally the classis of Delft gave it as its opinion (1614) that the only way to supply the need would be by founding a Missionary Seminary for the express training of missionaries. It suggested that it be founded at Leyden at first and then transferred to the Indies—a very far-sighted opinion. The first part of it was soon carried out, the last part not till over three centuries had elapsed when Kam founded a Seminary in Amboyna and later a seminary was founded at Depok, Java, by the Rhenish Society.

But still the Dutch moved forward with their proverbial slowness before doing anything. It required certain events to bring matters to a crisis. One was that the Governor of the East Indies sent home complaints of the fewness of ministers. Then finally the East India Company concluded to found a Missionary Seminary at Leyden and the Theological Faculty at Leyden was asked to arrange for its establishment. The University proposed a plan drawn up by Walaeus, who all along had been the moving spirit in missions. This plan gave, first, the reasons for the founding of such a seminary, and, second, a description of it. In the first, emphasis was laid on the choice of candidates, in the second, on their training. As to the first the candidate must be of age, have a certificate from his classis or consistory or from several reliable persons, and must undergo a year of probation before being fully received. For training he was to be placed in the house of the Regent, he was to practice self-control, fasting, prayer, visitation of the sick and do the work of a sick-comforter, an office common in the

Dutch Church. All these would prepare him for work among the heathen. Besides their ordinary studies the students were to be careful to gain a knowledge of the Jewish, Mohammedan and heathen religions so as to be able to meet these enemies in the colonies. They were also to study the Malay language so as to be able to speak to the natives. This broad, full plan satisfied the Directors of the East India Company and on April 1, 1622, it was decided to found such a Missionary Seminary.

They approached Prof. Walaeus to act as Regent. At the urgent request of the two curators and of the theological faculty he accepted. He had hesitated at first, because of the additional care and responsibility it would place on his household to receive and care for so many young men. But the Directors met this point by requiring the students, together with an elderly woman, to take care of their own rooms and laundry, thus relieving Mrs. Walaeus. They were also to be supplied with a nurse in case of sickness so that she would have no care. To relieve Walaeus of discipline as much as possible the students were admonished not to feast, swear, quarrel, visit tennis courts, or hotels, etc. They were also to put out the lights at 10 p. m., and go to bed. If visiting friends they were to return before 9 p. m.

All smoking was forbidden. This last may seem to us a strange rule for a nation so given to smoking as the Dutch. But it is to be remembered that tobacco smoking was brought into Europe in the 17th century and had not yet become common; indeed was outlawed as yet by good Christian society which then placed the debauchee, drunkard and smoker on the same level, and it was tabooed by the careful Dutch housewife who would not allow the "villainous stink and brimstone" in her clean ornamental dwelling. The student was also forbidden to engage himself in marriage. All these things the student had to bind himself to on entering the seminary. If he continued in any breaches of these rules he was expelled.

But Walaeus was as anxious for the spiritual development of the students as of the moral. They were to regularly attend the church services on Sunday and on weekdays when possible. Besides private devotion, they were to have a prayermeeting together every morning and evening. We thus see how carefully the plan of this seminary was arranged for the proper preparation of the students for their work.

The Seminary was founded in 1622, the very same year the Roman Catholic Church opened the great missionary institution of Rome, "The Society for the Propagation of Faith." How magnificent and splendid that, how weak and insignificant this, and yet by the twentieth century the movement set on foot by the latter had outstripped the Romish Propaganda, as Protestant Missions outstripped the Catholic in the nineteenth century. It is true that the missionary seminary at Leyden continued in existence but ten years, but it gave a beginning to Protestant Missions and an impulse that it never lost. It laid the foundation. From that time to this, the Protestant Church, even in the days of the greatest rationalism or deadest orthodoxy, has not been without its missionary among the heathen, a fact not true of Protestantism before; for nearly three quarters of a century had elapsed since the first Protestant Missionaries had gone to Brazil. There is an apostolic succession in foreign missions more real than that which comes from the Bishop's touch. From this school there came the Dutch Missions of the seventeenth century, followed in the eighteenth century by the Lutheran and Moravian Missions, and in Britain by Angelican and Dissenter,

The Reformed Church. 27

to be followed in the nineteenth century by a magnificent advance all along the line of denominations until they present a solid front of missionary advance in the twentieth century. Before this seminary was founded there had been a breach in Protestant missions among the heathen of over a half century, but since its founding there has been no break. The seminary lapsed but the holy fire it started is still burning brighter to-day than ever and shining brighter and brighter like the ascending sun, while Romish Propaganda is declining like the waning moon.

In ten years of its existence, this seminary sent forth (as far as it is possible to gain information from the meagre sources) about a dozen pupils, although the list is not complete. Jacob Vertrecht of Leyden matriculated September 22, 1625, and later went to Amboyna. Nicholas Molinaeus of Leyden was stationed in the Coromandel coast, India, in 1628. John Cavallarius, from Zeeland, one of the first pupils, like Molinaeus, died soon after entering upon his work in the East Indies. Michael Clarenbeek and William Holtenus labored in the Banda Islands. Abraham De Roy, or Roger, of Leyden, labored in Paliacate, and Robert Junius at Formosa. A list of other students as living in Walaeus's family is given as Jacob Tollens, of Bremen, John Cauelier, of Middlebush. George Candidius is also spoken of by De Roy, as also one Samuel Carlier (1629) of Middleburg, Anthony Van der Hagen, of Utrecht, (1629), the latter laboring in the East Indies. Some of these were found on the register of the Leyden University, but some evidently were special students under Walaeus' supervision. It is difficult to get at them exactly. Of those mentioned Robert Junius, the missionary to Formosa, was the most prominent and also George Candidius. Of the rest Molinaeus, one of the early pupils, did good work on the Cormandel coast where he preached in Portuguese and taught the Malays the fundamental truths of Christianity. Jacob Vertrecht's life is perhaps the fullest given. He left Holland in 1632 for Amboyna. He preached to the heathen in the Malay as easier for himself to speak and the natives to understand than the Amboyna language. In 1635 he had sixty-five converts of whom two were elders and two deacons. In the villages he had schools with more than sixty children whom he taught the Lord's Prayer, the Ten Commandments, and the twelve articles of faith. Every evening in each village evening-prayer was held, led by the teacher. He drew up a small catechism for them. He founded a school of ten boys for instruction in theology so that they might be able to teach others. He preached in Amboyna, Banda and Formosa.

But after being in existence for ten years this Missionary School at Leyden was given up. Why? The reason given by the East India Company was that by that time sufficient ministers could be found in Holland for their possessions and therefore such a school was unnecessary. But reading between the lines, there were doubtless other reasons which affected the Company. Some friction developed between the missionaries and the Company. The missionaries were earnest men. Walaeus had filled them with his own heart-earnestness for the salvation of the heathen. When the missionaries arrived in the colonies they were first of all disgusted by the immoralities of the Europeans there. When they were bold in preaching against gross sins, the government officials (some of them guilty) opposed them. If they urged any reforms the government stood in the way. As a result some of the missionaries became angry at the opposition they experienced and wanted to return home.

The government would also sometimes interfere with the rights of the ministers. Thus in 1632 Clarenbeek and Holtenus were laboring with much success in the Banda Islands when the governor received orders from his superiors always to send two representatives to the church gatherings and to demand that they should place in his hands all letters addressed to Batavia. When the consistories objected to this, they were forbidden to meet. This act undermined the influence of the missionaries and caused such a disturbance that they wanted to return. Vertrecht also came into collision with the governor who suspended him illegally (1636) but the consistory of Batavia restored him. The greatest controversy was about the independence of the congregations, the Company assuming unwarranted authority over them contrary to the customs of the Dutch Church at home. Another difficulty was caused by the Company urging laxity of discipline and thus discouraging the ministers.

The truth was that this seminary of Walaeus developed its pupils into a high spiritual state, far above the wishes of the Company; their earnest piety was too great for the worldly money-loving officials of the Company. Their zeal, too, for the salvation of the heathen resulted in successes more than the Company had expected or desired. But all this is only the greater tribute to Walaeus' piety and zeal (the influence of his personal piety must have been very great) and to the spiritual tone and education of this seminary. When the seminary was discontinued the Company gave Walaeus a gilded cup as a token of their appreciation of his work, but he has richer mead in the stars of his crown in heaven and in the lasting impulse given to missions by his seminary here.

Chapter III.

THE DUTCH REFORMED MISSIONARIES IN BRAZIL.

Nearly a century passed away after the French Reformed mission in Brazil had been broken up by the Jesuits who aimed to make America only a Catholic land. In 1621 the Dutch West India Company was incorporated and planted a colony at Pernambuco, the most eastern point of Brazil, twelve hundred miles north of Rio Janeiro. Its governor was one of the greatest generals in Holland, Count John Maurice, of Nassau-Siegen, "the honor of his age, the ornament of his house."

He was a German by birth, but like the princes of the family of Nassau, he had entered the Dutch service. He was an ardent member of the Reformed Church. He sailed from Holland October 25, 1636, accompanied by the prayers of the Dutch Christians that his company might save many from Romanism and from heathenism. He landed at Pernambuco January 23, 1637. As a wise governor he soon felt the need of increasing religious influence. He set a worthy example by regular attendance at church where he enjoyed the preaching of his learned court preacher, Francis Plante. Still true to his Dutch principles of religious liberty he did not persecute the Catholics. He soon felt the need of ministers and urgently requested the West India Company to send more ministers from Holland who should also act as missionaries to the natives. In 1637 eight ministers were sent. They evangelized in Dutch, French, Portuguese and English. Soller and Polhemius preached at Olinda; Poelius at Tamarica; Rathelarius (an Englishman) at Parahiba; in the province of St. Augustine, Stetinus proclaimed the gospel, as did Eduardi, at Serihaen. In the province of Maragnana the Gospel was also preached. These missionaries seemed to have had the true missionary spirit.

It is to be noticed that these men already in the infancy of Protestant missions used one of its first principles, namely, preaching the gospel in the native tongue. In their efforts to evangelize they were ably supported by Count John Maurice and his court preacher. They found that the Jesuits had done very superficial work. The great difference between the Protestants and Catholics is that the Protestants give the natives the Bible while the Catholics do not. All the Jesuits did was to teach the natives to recite the Creed and the Lord's Prayer. The Dutch ministers aimed at higher results. They learned their language so as to preach to them. Davilus was the first to do this. Doriflarius was eloquent in both the Portuguese and Brazilian, and translated the Catechism into the Tapuya dialect—the first Protestant catechism in the language of the Indians.

This colony was also noted for its fair dealings with the Indians. Long before William Penn, Count John Maurice introduced it into Brazil. He placed a Dutchman in each village who protected the natives so that they were not cheated by the whites but were paid for their goods. The natives so highly honored the Count that one of their chiefs presented him with a costly dish which he later presented to the Reformed Church at Siegen, Germany. In 1645 he returned to Holland bringing not less than twenty-five tons of gold with him and was received with high honors there. The Portuguese soon after destroyed the Dutch colony, but the Dutch, though driven out of Brazil, later acquired Dutch Guiana in South America.*

Thus, although the Reformed Church was

---

*There are now about 7,000 Reformed in Guiana.

crushed out of Brazil, yet in these two colonies, French and Dutch, she could boast the first Protestant missionaries; the first missionary martyrs; the first Indian Catechism; the first Protestant Church organization in America in classis and synods and the first attempt at fair dealing with the Indians.

REV. ROBERT JUNIUS.

Chapter IV.

THE DUTCH REFORMED MISSION IN FORMOSA.

THE CRUCIFIXION OF THE REFORMED.

The Reformed Church of Holland did a great work for missions in the seventeenth century which is unknown to English readers, yet of great interest to every member of the Reformed Church. One of her most successful missions was on the island of Formosa, southeast of China.*

In 1624 the Dutch East India Company began trading with Formosa. The Dutch in their zeal for the spread of Christ's kingdom, sent the missionary along with the merchant. Two Scripture readers (more literally Sick-Comforters) were first sent. One of them soon returned but the other, Dirk Lauwrenzoon, continued the work till May, 1626. The first minister who arrived there was George Candidius who landed May 4, 1627. He at once began very zealously to learn their language so as to preach to them. In his letter written December,

---

*An early record of this work has come down to us written by the faithful missionary, Rev. Robert Junius, which was translated into English and printed in London in 1650. It was recently reprinted and it is entitled "Missionary Success in Formosa," by Campbell, published by Trubner, London, two volumes.

1628, he says: "I have used great diligence to learn the language of the people and to instruct them in the Christian faith and have succeeded so far that a fortnight before Christmas of the present year there were 128 persons who knew the Lord's Prayer and were able to explain in the most satisfactory manner the principal articles of the Christian faith but who for certain reasons have not yet been baptized.

After Candidius had been there two years, Rev. Robert Junius arrived. He preached for two years in Dutch, but being moved by a great desire for the conversion of the heathen, he with great difficulty, learned their rude language. His success was astonishing. Men of all ranks and conditions were converted. Fifty natives were trained to teach, who had six hundred scholars. Churches were planted in twenty-three towns. The Dutch Missionaries took pains to furnish them with suitable catechisms, Scripture translations, etc. The headquarters of the mission was at Sakan.*

In 1631 Mr. Candidius was called away to go to Batavia, in Java. His heart, however, was in the mission work at Formosa and he returned again two

---

*Sakan has since developed into the large Chinese city of Taiwanfoo.

years later. The Lord so greatly blessed the missionary labors for two years that by 1635 they had received seven hundred adults into the Church. So hopeful was the outlook that they reported to the Dutch Governor in 1636 that at least fifteen additional ministers would be needed to take possession of the fields that were opening up to them.

But in 1637 Mr. Junius was left alone as Mr. Candidius returned to Holland, after having labored in Formosa for ten years. Yet he writes encouragingly in a letter dated October 23, 1640. He says: "A few days ago we visited five villages, where we preached and baptized many of the inhabitants, who had been under instruction for some time. I found them to be very zealous, coming regularly, morning and evening to the house of the schoolmasters, to be instructed until they were able to repeat fluently the prayers, etc. The largest number of persons who received baptism was at Soulang, one hundred and twenty persons, among them a grown-up person who had never been instructed, but who earnestly begged to be baptized, saying, 'Examine me, for I wish to be baptized.' He answered so well the questions put to him, that it delighted his hearers, and the next day he was baptized. Up to the present time one thousand and seventy persons have been baptized at Soulang." In twenty-three villages he induced the people to abandon their idols. In six villages he baptized upwards of fifty-four hundred persons.

In 1640 another missionary, Rev. John Bavius, came, while Mr. Junius was granted a leave of absence after ten years' faithful service. When he arrived at Batavia he was asked whether he would be willing to return to Formosa or go to Holland. He said he would be willing to go back to Formosa provided the Dutch Governor there would be prevented from hindering their work. The assurance having been given him, he returned with two other missionaries in 1641. In 1646 Rev. Mr. Bavius still lived at the village of Soulang, having under his direction four other villages. Mr. Van Breen was laboring at Favorlang and the neighboring villages. Mr. Happartius, who went out in 1644, was stationed at the castle Zeelandia, the Dutch fort on the south side of the island, where he conducted Dutch services and also attended to the natives in the neighboring villages. Mr. Olaf, a most acceptable candidate of theology, labored among the southern villages, but as his parish was entirely too long, extending from

The Reformed Church. 41

Favorlang to Pangsoia, he earnestly asked for an assistant. In 1647 Mr. Bavius died, and Mr. Van Breen returned to Holland.

But at that time God raised up another man to go to Formosa in his place. Rev. Daniel Gravius, a prominent minister at Batavia, a man of great talents and influential with the government, felt himself called upon to go. In vain did his congregation and friends try to change his decision, but he would not be dissuaded. He left for Formosa amid the tears of his sorrowing congregation. He remained in Formosa four years, and was of great service there, because of his great linguistic abilities, in aiding them in the language. He then returned to Batavia to his old congregation and finally to Holland. But as late as January 2, 1662, he still showed great interest in the Formosan mission, for he published his "Formulary of Christianity," a carefully and learned work of 300 pages, in which the Dutch and Formosan languages are printed in parallel columns. In 1653 the Church affairs at Formosa were still reported to the Dutch government as being very prosperous, and a call for new laborers was issued, but it seemed difficult to get many to go to such a distant island. Still, some were sent.

But in 1661 political dangers began to threaten this prosperous mission. The Ming dynasty in China was supplanted by the present Manchu-Tartar dynasty in 1644. Koxinga, one of the most daring spirits of that age, refused allegiance to the new dynasty. He collected a large fleet, which swept the seas, and had tens of thousands of adherents on the land. But with all his bravery, he was not able to stem the tide of the Tartar leaders. He was driven back in China, until he was compelled to leave China and seek some islands as a refuge for his forces. Unfortunately, he turned his eyes toward the fertile island of Formosa. With his coming the sad persecutions of the Reformed missions began. In 1661 Koxinga landed at Formosa and summoned the Dutch garrison at Zeelandia to surrender immediately, or else they would be put to death by fire and the sword. But the Dutchmen are not accustomed to surrender so quickly and they refused. He then began the siege of Fort Zeelandia. It lasted nine months. During this time the Dutch tried in every way to strengthen their position, but the enemy very vigorously blockaded them, while at the same time they ravaged the country far and near, cruelly inflicting terrible cruelties on the natives

The Reformed Church.   43

and the Reformed missions. Especially did they single out ministers and school teachers, who were threatened with every sort of indignity, even death itself.

The journal of John Kruyf, kept during the siege, gives sketches of these sufferings. He says: "Van Druyvendal and a schoolmaster named Franz Van der Voorn, with three other Dutchmen, were brought to Sinkang. The first two were crucified at Sakam. Rev. Mr. Hambroek finally gained Koxinga's permission to offer up a prayer for them. After they had hung on their crosses for three days, they were carried, still alive, on the crosses to Sinkang, and here the crosses were again planted in the ground until the sufferers died." The same journal gives a further description of this Reformed schoolmaster. It says: "The interpreter Druyvendal and a young schoolmaster had each been fastened to a cross by having nails driven through their hands and calves of their legs, and another nail driven into their backs. In this sad condition they hung for three or four days, and then died after meat and drink had been withheld from them all that time." These were Reformed crucifixions. These Reformed were crucified like their Saviour, who was crucified for them. The Chinese, under Koxinga, forced all the inhabitants who had taken Christian names to take other names again, and threatened severe punishment if this command was not obeyed.

A very touching incident is told by Neihoff, which reveals a hero in a Reformed minister, who is worthy of being placed alongside of Regulus in ancient Roman history. He was Rev. Mr. Hambroek, who was sent by Koxinga to the Dutch governor to propose terms for the surrender of the fort, and to tell the governor that in case of refusal, vengeance would be taken on the Dutch captives of Koxinga. Hambroek came into the Dutch fort, being forced to leave his wife and children behind as hostages, which sufficiently proved that if he failed in his errand, he had nothing but death to expect from Koxinga. Yet when he entered the Dutch fort, instead of trying to urge the garrison to surrender, he encouraged them to a brave defense by hopes of relief, assuring them that Koxinga had lost many of his best ships and soldiers, and had begun to be weary of the siege. When he had ended, the council of war refused to surrender, and as to himself, they left it to his choice to stay with them in the fort or return to Koxinga's army, where he

could expect nothing but present death. Every
one entreated him to stay. He had two daughters in the fort who hung on his neck, overwhelmed
with grief and tears at seeing their father go where
he knew he must be sacrificed by the merciless enemy. But he represented to them that having left his
wife and two other children in the camp as hostages,
nothing but death could attend them if he did not
return. So unlocking himself from his daughters'
arms, he returned to Koxinga's camp, telling them at
parting that he hoped he might prove serviceable to
his poor fellow-prisoners. On his return Koxinga
received his answer sternly, and then enraged, he
caused it to be rumored that the prisoners were in-
citing the people of Formosa to rise against him,
and ordered that all the Dutch male prisoners should
be put to death. This was done and some were beheaded, others killed in a more barbarous manner.
Five hundred were put to death, fifty or sixty of
them being stripped quite naked and buried alive together in a hole. The women and children were not
spared, many of them being slain, though some of
the best were preserved as slaves. Among the slain
were four Reformed ministers—Hambroek, Mus,
Winsem and Ampzingius, and many schoolmasters,

who were beheaded, and who thus became martyrs.

Meanwhile the garrison in the fort were enduring very great sufferings. Shut in by land and sea they suffered great want. And with the famine came sickness, so that they lost by disease and the sword 1600 men. They were finally compelled to surrender at the beginning of 1662, when the enemy allowed them to depart in their only remaining ship. The journal thus says: "Who can without tears remember the unexpected destruction and ruin of so many families and of nearly thirty ministers, partly in their lives, partly in their fortunes?" The next year when Mr. Bert arrived with a Dutch fleet, he found Koxinga's son still ruling, who said that the Rev. J. de Leonardis and others were still at Sakam, and that he would be willing to open the island to the Dutch for trade and give them a settlement at Tamsui, if they would help him against the Tartars. But nothing came of these negotiations, so the Reformed who were really held as prisoners had to remain there in dreary exile, without any communication with Christian civilization and home, until September 2, 1684, twenty-three years afterwards. Then some of them escaped, of whom Alexander Schravenbroek, during his twenty-two years of imprison-

The Reformed Church. 47

ment, had so fully mastered the language that the government engaged him as their interpreter.

Thus this promising Reformed mission was broken up. Valentyn gives the names of thirty-five Reformed ministers, as having labored there a longer or shorter time, the most prominent of whom was Robert Junius. Thus the mission, which in the nearly forty years of its existence had grown to 6,000 members, was scattered to the winds. The only thing that remained of the mission was a copy of the Gospel of St. Matthew, in the Formosan dialect, and that is to be found in the University of Leyden, Holland. This was about being printed for them when the Chinese invaders entered their land in 1661. It was prepared by the learned Gravius.

The island was closed to foreigners and Christians two hundred years ago, until the treaty of Tien-tsin (1860) opened it again. The Presbyterian Church of England began mission work again there in 1865. They were followed seven years later by the Presbyterian Church of Canada, of whose number the brave Junius finds a worthy successor in Rev. Dr. Geo. L. Mackay, who has well been styled "a modern apostle." There are now more than seventy congregations on the island, some of them in the villages occupied by the people whose ancestors were members and office bearers in that early martyr Reformed Church of Formosa. Thus in the village of Toasia there is a self-supporting congregation of one hundred and sixteen members. The young pastor there is a lineal descendant of the chief, who brought the tribes under subjection of the Chinese. Thus the martyr Reformed Church of Formosa is again rising, Phoenix-like, from her ashes, and that island is seeing the strange sight of natives casting away their idols and coming to Christ in that splendid mission of the Presbyterian Church of Canada.

The Dutch Reformed also had other missions in the East Indies—in Java, Amboyna, Ceylon and the Molucca Islands. In 1722 there were 424,392 converts. But unfortunately, the work was often superficially done. The number of missionaries was too few, so that their work lacked depth and permanence. Still a beginning was made which came to blessed fruitage in some districts in the nineteenth century.

BOOK II.

DR. THEODOSIUS VANDERKEMP.

THE REFORMED IN AFRICA.
Chapter I.
THEODOSIUS VANDERKEMP.

A MODERN apostle was Theodosius Vanderkemp—at least he has never been surpassed since the days of the apostles in consecration and self-denial. He was a Dutchman, born in 1747, at Rotterdam, where his father was pastor of the Dutch Reformed Church. He took a five years' course of training at the University of Leyden, and became a physician. Later he exchanged his position of physician for that of a soldier under the Prince of Orange for sixteen years, where he rose to be captain of the horse. Then owing to a difference between the Prince of Orange and himself, he left the army and returned to the practice of medicine. He went to Edinburgh where he distinguished himself by his knowledge of the sciences and modern languages, and then settled at Rotterdam and by the practice of medicine he made a great deal of money.

But a sudden event changed his life in 1791. He was sailing on the river near Dort, when a violent storm arose and a water-spout broke over his boat, by which it was instantly upset. His wife and daughter were instantly drowned before his eyes, and he was brought to the point of death. Clinging to the boat, he was carried down stream nearly a mile, as no one dared, in so dreadful a storm, to venture to his aid. A vessel then lying at the port of Dort was by a mysterious providence driven from her moorings and floated toward the part of the river where he was just ready to sink, and the sailors took him from the wreck. His proud heart was completely broken by this providence. As a young man he had lived a dissolute life, but since his marriage he had lived an outwardly moral life. Yet he had imbibed that spirit of rationalism so common in his day. He did not believe in the Bible, and denied the divinity of Christ. But his soul, now completely broken up by the accident, could not find rest till it found rest in Christ. Slowly and with many struggles he fought his way back to faith—a brand plucked from the burning, and destined to become a burning and shining light for the Gospel. The Book and the Saviour whom he once despised, now became his hope and treasure.

About this time he came across the report of a

great London missionary meeting containing sermons and addresses, etc., and one text, "Curse ye Meroz," entered his soul. Falling on his knees, he cried, "O, Lord Jesus, here am I; Thou knowest I have no will of my own since I devoted myself to Thy service." He at once offered himself to the London Missionary Society,* though over fifty years of age.

He was appointed to South Africa, and was ordained November 3, 1797. But before leaving the Netherlands, in order that his influence might remain behind him, he organized two missionary societies, one at Rotterdam and the other in Friesland, the former of which has become the well known Netherlands Missionary Society, which now has missions in the East Indies with about 20,000 communicants. In 1798 he sailed with three others, one of whom, Kicherer, like himself, seems to have been a missionary from the Dutch Reformed Church also. Vanderkemp did not wait until he arrived at Africa before he began missionary work. On the vessel in which they sailed, there were a number of con-

---

*The London Missionary Society, like all the missionary societies of its day, was undenominational.

victs on their way to the penal colony in Australia. He at once became interested in them, and addressed them with such power that there was an awakening in the ship, and through it many of them were led to change their lives. When the time came for the convicts to separate from Vanderkemp at the Cape of Good Hope, nearly all of these strong, wicked men shed tears. Perhaps some of them had never received a word of help and kindness before. He arrived at Capetown in March, 1799.

At Capetown Vanderkemp at once began work. He started among the natives, the slaves, Mohammedans and Hottentots, although he tried to awaken a deeper interest in missions among the Europeans. In May, 1799, he left Capetown for the interior with Mr. Edmonds. He traveled northeastward, aiming to work among the Caffres. These were a very different race from the Hottentots. They were a courageous, strong and warlike people, with high foreheads and black eyes, while the Hottentots had low foreheads and were menial, and seemed destined to be slaves. The Caffres were cruel to their enemies, and would wait long for vengeance. They included the Bechuana, Basuto and Zulu tribes. They had long and bloody wars with the natives and the

English. In the last war with the English, one of the tribes, the Zulus, defeated the English, and the Prince Imperial, the son of the Emperor Louis Napoleon, lost his life. They were, therefore, very brave, but dangerous to labor among. It has been supposed by some that because they do not eat swine's flesh, and practice circumcision, they are distant descendants of the Jews who emigrated from the north. Through a country full of dangers he pushed and finally arrived on the border of this warlike tribe.

After a month's travel he was brought before their king, Geika, unarmed, and without any attendants but a few Hottentots. The Caffres at first thought he was a spy. Some slaves and criminals who had fled from the colony, aroused suspicion among the Caffres against him. But it happened that on his way he stopped at the farm of a Dutch colonist named Beer. Mr. Beer had that very day buried a little girl. The arrival of the missionary was a balm to his heart. "O Lord," he cried in his prayer at family devotion that night, "Thou hast sent me a trial, but Thou hast at the same time granted me a great joy in answering my long continued prayer for a missionary. Thou art faithful to Thy promises." It is said that through Mr. Beer's intercession the chief gave Vanderkemp a place to live in. Geika had given him permission to pitch his tent but advised him to leave on account of the unsettled state of the times. He was not safe from wild beasts and wilder men, who at times closely watched his dwelling.

Various stories are told of the way in which renegades from the colony would stir up the chief against him. One of the Dutch farmers went to the Caffre chief and made him believe that Vanderkemp would try to poison him by giving him brandy with water in it. The chief, taking a company of armed men, went to the missionary, fully determined to kill him as soon as he offered him anything to drink. He seated himself near his wagon and began to talk with Vanderkemp. Hours passed away, and still the brandy did not appear. Tired of waiting, the chief went away, but soon returned and asked, "Haven't you any brandy?" "I have not," answered the missionary, without a suspicion of the danger he had passed through, "and never expect to have any." "Then they have deceived me," cried the chief, throwing himself at the feet of the missionary. "I see that you are a good man. You do not wish to kill me." Permission having been given, he opened a station and school. The chief, though he disliked him, yet appealed to his aid. When the country was desolated by a long drought, Geika sent for Vanderkemp, so as to obtain rain through him. Fearing that if he did so it would be attributed to magical art, like that of the professional rain-makers of the heathen, Vanderkemp refused. But the chief sent a second messenger, who told him the king said, "It is cruel to treat the Caffres thus. You know if you will only go on your knees and hide your face in your hands, we will have as much rain as we want." "So be it then," said Vanderkemp. He remembered Elijah's prayers for rain, and he began to pray. The God of Elijah answered and rain came in torrents for several days. The chief sent a messenger with many thanks to him, but gave him a compliment that made him smile. "Another time," said the chief, "be a little more moderate. This time you have almost drowned us. Here, however, is a fat ox as the proof of my gratitude." Vanderkemp peremptorily refused to receive the ox. But one of the scoundrel whites who infested the country, conceived the idea of making a good thing at Vanderkemp's expense. He met in the woods the

Caffre taking the ox back to the chief. "What?" said he, when the native told him the story how the ox was brought back to the chief. "What, one ox— one single ox for such a splendid rain as that? It is an insult. Let Geika at once send me six oxen like this. I will take it on myself to present them to the missionary. You will see that they are accepted." The chief forwarded the six oxen to this officious middle man, and it hardly need be added that neither Geika nor the missionary ever heard of them again.

Vanderkemp found his life constantly in danger from such men as these adventurers who accompanied the retailers of brandy, and were marauding among the natives, falling on them most cruelly unawares. Such men could not forgive Vanderkemp for the love he had toward the Hottentots and Caffres. More than once they attempted his life, but God preserved him. The Caffres saw his danger, and also noted his safety and came to regard him as a sacred being, who had power with the invisible God, before whom they so often saw him pray. His companion, Mr. Edmonds, having left, he continued alone in Caffreland for over a year. Then Geika, becoming jealous of the growing power of

Christianity, ordered him away. He left, followed by sixty converts. Thus ended his work among the Caffres, whose hearts seemed like stone, and yet it did not end. He sowed good seed, for thirty years afterwards an aged woman was admitted to the Church who had received the Gospel from his lips. But the most important result was that he, with his wonderful skill at languages, prepared a dictionary of the Caffre language. The London Missionary Society said that he had done more in sixteen months than many missionaries did in a lifetime. He only opened the door into Caffreland for missionaries younger than himself. And up to a few years ago, in all regions occupied by Caffres, the natives who embraced Christianity were frequently called Ma Yankana, meaning, "the men of Vanderkemp."

Vanderkemp, having been compelled to leave Caffreland, arrived with his converts in May, 1801, at Graff Reinet. He was offered the pastorate of the Dutch Church there, but refused, for he felt that his mission was to minister to and save the poor Hottentots. He soon collected a colony of two hundred. Buildings were erected at Graff Reinet for the mission and it became a permanent station. But the whites soon became jealous and charged him with teaching the slaves and heathen, so that they might become the equals of the whites. He saw that it would be safer to have the Hottentots go out from among the whites into a separate colony, and after many struggles, he gained permission to found another colony. The government granted him land near Algoa Bay. A part of his congregation occupied it early in 1802. When the governor visited it that year, although it was not a complete success, he was so much impressed with the good it was doing, as well as the danger of the location, for the wild Hottentots had repeatedly attacked them, that he urged them to occupy Fort Frederick, which had just been given up by its garrison. So to be safe from the opposition of the colonists and from the attacks of plundering Hottentots he went with three hundred Hottentots to that fort. His work now became more encouraging, as several Hottentots applied for baptism. He was so ill with rheumatism at the time that he had to baptize them as he lay on his couch.

The country then passed from the rule of the English into the hands of the Dutch. It was expected that they would be prejudiced against the mission, because the Boers hated the Hottentots. But the governor soon discovered how much good Vanderkemp was doing, and gave him his assistance in forming a new mission. He granted them a station at Kooboo, where they commenced a station named Bethelsdorp (seven miles north of the bay), which was founded in June, 1803. This place had little to favor it. The soil was poor, and there was hardly enough water for domestic purposes. They could not irrigate, and so they could only farm with difficulty. Five years after, they wrote to the directors of the Mission that they had been without bread for a long time, and did not expect to procure any for three or four months, nor had they any vegetables. And yet they took this desert place, and under the blessing of God, after a long time, made it blossom like the rose.

The Hottentots at once began to gather round Vanderkemp, when they found that they had a friend and a sympathizer in him. The progress of his scholars there was astonishing; and, above all, their faculty in acquiring religious knowledge, when one considers their native stupidity, was wonderful. In the first year twenty-two were baptized. From this time on till the reoccupation by the British, the work was carried on with great vigor by Vanderkemp. In 1807 great religious interest was manifested and an out-station at Steurmanns Krall established. By 1810 the population of Bethelsdorp was 1,000, so rapidly did the mission grow. Thus his work prospered.

Some very beautiful stories are told of his work. Cupido, a Hottentot, was remarkable for swearing, lying, fighting and drunkenness, which often laid him on a sick bed. At such times he would resolve on reformation, but when he became well again, he would forget all his vows. He was sometimes afraid of God, though he knew little of Him. He was providentially led to Graff Reinet, where he heard Vanderkemp declare that Jesus Christ, the Son of God, could save sinners from their sins. He said within himself, "That is what I want. That is what I want." He went to the missionary and asked that he might become acquainted with this Jesus. He then told all that he had found One who could save him from his sins. He not only became a believer, but through a sermon of Vanderkemp, also a devoted and successful missionary. Another interesting case was that of Lentze, a Caffre woman. She was a convert, and was remarkable for her integrity of life and her constancy and fervor in prayer. In her last illness she spent almost day and night in communion with Christ. One morning she sent for Vanderkemp, requesting him to give her farewell to all the people of God, and then desired to be placed in the open air. When he and his servant had carried her out of doors, she said, "Now I will go to my Lord," and expired.

Dr. Vanderkemp had his peculiarities and eccentricities; and yet they reveal his wonderfully consecrated spirit. He was a man of great frugality, and carried the carelessness of his person to the extremest limits. He never wore a hat in South Africa. On one occasion, when some new trick that his enemies played on his Hottentots, compelled him to go up to Cape Town to appeal to the authorities, he had to buy a hat. But even then he did not use it as a head-covering, but held it in his hands behind his back. The street boys took advantage of his forgetfulness, and amused themselves from behind by filling it with gravel. The doctor soon discovered by its weight that it was no longer empty, and simply emptied it. But even then he did not put it on his head, but bareheaded went on his walk. He held rigid views about a missionary's life. His maxim was that a missionary should own only the clothes he had on, and that he should conform himself to the food of the natives. He insisted that the London Society ought to allow only $150 a year to its workers. He did not do this merely from a notion of economy, but he held that if you would raise the natives up to your level, you must go down to theirs in everything that was not wrong. This principle has since been proved a false one, yet it revealed his consecration and self-denial for God. It meant the giving up of civilization in order to save the blacks. It is said that on one occasion an English diplomatic officer visited him in Caffreland and found him brick-making without a hat, and in a costume as light as that of the natives. In his devotion to his principles he went so far as to redeem a black slave girl and then marry her, so that he might gain the entire sympathy of the blacks, and thus bring them to Christ. She was a converted Hottentot, who remained to the end uneducated, so different from himself that it caused him a great deal of trouble. So great was his love for the poor Hottentots that he said: "I should not fear to offer my life for the last child among them."

Still, with all his eccentricities, he was a wonderfully consecrated man. He was a close student of

God's Word. The Hottentots preserve many stories of his studies. They would say that in his travels when at evening they would unyoke the oxen and were preparing the doctor's meal he would go and seat himself some distance among the bushes with paper and pencil in hand. There he gave himself to prayer and meditation. They used to hear him say sometimes, "Lord, I do not understand this point, this word." A moment afterwards he would say, "I see it a little better now, but not enough. Enlighten me." And then often, after a moment of silence he cried, "Oh, now I understand; thanks, thanks, Lord." Then, in spite of the darkness he would begin to write, and his pencil would fly over the paper. He was prayful, and yet he did not believe in being always on his knees. Prayer without ceasing meant prayer in the spirit, rather than prayer in the act. One day while he was traversing a forest in Caffraria with a young missionary suddenly a band of warriors appeared in full armor, making motions in an alarming manner. The new missionary, whose carriage was following his, got out and ran to him, begging him to stop and ask God's protection. But Vanderkemp said, "My friend, didn't you pray this morning? Let us go on."

The cruelties which the poor Hottentots suffered from the whites caused feelings of deepest pity in his heart. It is said that within three years he had paid no less than $5,000 to redeem slaves. Through him and the other missionaries the Hottentots were finally delivered from their oppressions. When Cape Colony was under control of the Dutch, it is said the Boers earnestly requested General Janssen, the governor, to expel Vanderkemp and the other missionaries, because they were trying to civilize and Christianize the Hottentots. The governor indignantly refused, and even went so far as to try to have justice done to the Hottentots on the frontiers, because he had confidence in the missionaries. This fact ought to be mentioned, for it has been generally supposed that the Dutch were against the missionaries, but here their governor protected them. Vanderkemp was called on again and again to defend these persecuted Hottentots. For the Hottentots were very cruelly treated along the frontier. Rev. Mr. Read asserted to the directors of the London Missionary Society that 100 murders were brought to the knowledge of Vanderkemp and himself, and yet there was no redress. Dr. Vanderkemp became thus the great champion of the black race in South Africa, the Wilberforce of South Africa. Twice he had to go personally all the way to Cape Town to testify for them. Almost his last service was to go and testify in the courts at Cape Town against their wrongs.

He was under appointment of the London Missionary Society to go to Madagascar, and start a new mission there, when he suddenly died at Cape Town, December 15, 1811. His last words were: "It is all good." Thus, after 13 years of missionary work, he went to his rest. The Lord had prepared for him a better country than Madagascar. But his station at Bethelsdorp continued to prosper until it had, in 1889, raised up more than a hundred native preachers and brought 6,000 souls into the church and won by its instruction 30,000 adherents. The traveler who now visits it will find instead of Hottentot hovels, well built houses, a church, a school, a printing press and all kinds of mechanics. The ignorant Hottentots, under the influence of Christianity, have developed into noble men and women. In 1842, poor as they were, they gathered together as much as $480.00 for missions. After such a change one can well say, "If any man is in Christ, he is a new creature." The

Hottentots, almost the lowest of humanity, were by Vanderkemp's labors and through Christianity developed into equals of any.

Such was Vanderkemp—a most consecrated man. The Reformed Church—indeed, any other Church—has never raised up a more spiritually-minded, self-denying, consecrated missionary than he. One who was well acquainted with his work pays the following eloquent tribute to his life. He says that "for combining natural talents, extensive learning, elevated piety, ardent zeal, disinterested benevolence, unshaken perseverance and unfeigned humility he has not been equalled since the days of the apostles." No less an authority than the Rev. Dr. Moffat, the famous missionary to South Africa, the father-in-law of Livingston, says of him: "He came from the university to teach the alphabet to the poor, naked Hottentot and Caffre; from the society of nobles to associate with beings of the lowest grade of humanity; from stately mansions to the filthy hovel of the greasy African; from the army to instruct the fierce savage in the tactics of a heavenly warfare under the banner of the Prince of Peace; from the study of medicine to become a guide to the Balm of Gilead and the physician there; and finally from a life of earthly honor and ease to be exposed to perils of waters, of robbers, of his own countrymen, of the heathen, in the city, in the wilderness." He was a faint type and eloquent copy of his Master, who, though He was rich, for our sake became poor, who gave up the happiness and blessed society of heaven to come down to earth and live among sinful men, in order to save them. He, with Schmidt of the Moravians, was one of the first laborers for the regeneration of Africa. He was the forerunner of Moffat and Livingston, and prepared the way for their later triumphs. Thus his prayer when he built the first hut in Caffreland that "From under his roof the seed of the Gospel might spread through all Africa," was fulfilled. For all the wonderful changes that are taking place in the Dark Continent of Africa today may have said to have Vanderkemp as one of their starting points. He being dead, yet speaketh. And as thousands of these black Hottentots, washed white in the blood of the Lamb, shall take their place around God's throne in heaven, they will come as the trophies of the man, who, like his Master, gave up all in order to win them to Christ. "They that be wise, shall shine as the brightest of the firmament, and they that turn many to righteousness, as the stars forever and ever."

Chapter II.
EUGENE CASALIS.

One of the most consecrated of missionaries was Eugene Casalis, the French missionary to South Africa. On November 21, 1812, he was born of Huguenot parents at Orthez in southwestern France, where Viret, the Reformer of the sixteenth century, had taught theology. More than once had his ancestors suffered for their Reformed faith, for they belonged to the persecuted Church of the Desert. Indeed, the house of his grandfather had been one of the retreats of the Huguenot pastors, in those times of danger. There a window five feet from the ground opened into a vineyard, which opened into a woods beyond, thus providing a way of escape. Young Eugene used to rejoice to hear his grandmother tell how she had on one occasion aided a Reformed pastor to escape. He was conferring with her husband, when suddenly a breathless messenger burst in on them, telling them that the dragoons were on hand. The pastor quietly retired through the window to the woods, while she shut the door and began to wind thread. The dragoons soon arrived and demanded admission. She bravely replied: "Sir, I shall not open the door until you have shown me your orders." Fortunately the captain had forgotten them. So all that he could do was to stamp and storm outside. By and by when she felt that the pastor had gotten to a safe distance, she opened the door, saying: "Sir, my door is closed against everybody who endeavors to force it, unless authorized by the king; but it is opened to those, who, like you, have need of refreshment and repose." The dragoons immediately searched the house from cellar to garret, and found, not the fugitive pastor, but on their return a delicious repast prepared for them with true French hospitality.

Heir to such blood and such memories, Eugene easily became a hero. To his grandmother who told the story, he owed his first drawings to religion. As early as his ninth year his friends had marked him out for the ministry. But the missionary spirit was already beginning to work within the boy, for he relates how he wept over the story of two little Africans. His impressions were deepened by the earnest ministry of Rev. Mr. Pyt, one of the most godly and zealous of the French pastors, who preached at Bayonne, where Casalis lived. One day Mr. Pyt said to him: "Eugene, you are fifteen years old. It is time we know what you are going to be." He immediately replied: "I shall not tell you what I wish to be, but what I shall be,—a missionary." His pastor's heart greatly rejoiced at the decision; and so Eugene was sent to the Mission House at Paris.

One of the brightest jewels in the coronet of missions is the French mission in Southern Africa. The Paris Missionary Society was organized in November, 1822. France was entering upon a new era after Napoleon's defeat; and already less than ten years after his overthrow this society was formed. It was organized on an undenominational basis, but as most of the French Protestants were Reformed, it was of a prevailingly Reformed consciousness. Kalkar, in his excellent "History of Missions," calls it the French Reformed Missionary Society. It is now more prevailingly Reformed than at its beginning, for most of the Lutherans of France were lost to that country by the loss of Alsace and Lorraine; and now almost all its supporters and missionaries are from the old Huguenot Church. In 1828 Dr. Philip, that burning missionary herald of the Gospel in South Africa, happened to visit Paris, and urged them to choose South Africa as their mission field. They acted on his advice, sending out, in 1829, three missionaries—Rolland, Lemue and Bisseaux. This was the first time that the French Protestant Church had seen the spectacle of an appointment of missionaries for about 270 years, when Coligny sent two missionaries to Brazil.

The students of the Mission House were prepared for the foreign work by doing home missionary work in that great city. They had a chapel in a wretched quarter of the city where Casalis served his apprenticeship for his life-work among the savages. It happened that about this time cholera broke out. And one morning at the mission service as Casalis was offering prayer that God might guard them from the plague, but especially prepare them to die, suddenly a man fell over in the congregation. Casalis rushed from the pulpit and held the man in his arms while he writhed in the agonies of cholera. Two hours later the man died, and Casalis buried him the next day. Such labors, however, were only preparing him for his future work in South Africa.

It was expected that he would be sent to Algiers, which the French government had lately acquired, but it was soon decided that he should go to South Africa. So he went among his friends, bidding them good bye. Many of them, expecting never to see him again, lifted their finger to heaven as they said: "Adieu till we meet in heaven." His father clasped him to his bosom, saying: "I will never see you again," a prophecy which, alas, was fulfilled, for his father died soon after. Having been ordained at Paris, October 18, 1832, he finally, after a long and eventful voyage, arrived at Cape Colony, in South Africa.

When the first missionaries of this society had arrived in South Africa, they were joyfully received by the French who had settled there after the Revocation of the Edict of Nantes had driven them out of France, and they insisted that one of these French missionaries should remain and evangelize among them. Mr. Bisseaux was therefore left among them. He settled in Wagonmaker's Valley, forty miles northeast of the Cape Town, and began preaching the gospel to the Hottentots who were slaves of the farmers. So great was his success that within a year and a half ten were baptized. His work was transferred to Wellington and in 1875 there was a church there of 350 members and 200 children. Thus even before they had started a mission to the heathen in the interior, the missionaries were permitted to plant one centre of light right in the midst of the colony.

But the other two missionaries pressed on to the northeast to preach the gospel to the heathen. They then found themselves in the land of a cruel chief, Moselekatsi. They had hardly begun to collect materials to build, when war-like messengers appeared, commanding them to appear before the chief. As it was not prudent that all should go, for fear that none might return, Pelissier went alone, his servants declaring that he would never return. But though guarded with spears all the way, he received a more cordial welcome from the chief than he expected, and in a few days was permitted to return. But he had hardly returned before all the missionaries were ordered to appear before the chief. Word came to them from friends that they must not go, as the chief had decided on their ruin. They decided on flight.

So when Casalis arrived in Africa he was astonished to find that the mission already established by their society had been broken up, but Providence was opening up another and far better field for them. Here he and his two fellow-missionaries, Arbousset and Gosellin, were gladly received, especially by the Huguenots whose ancestors had emigrated there

The Reformed Church.

during the previous century. But his work was not among them, but in the "regions beyond."

How wonderfully God prepares the field for the workers as well as the workers for the field. For it happened that just before the time that these missionaries arrived at the Cape, the chief of the Basutos heard from a Hottentot of the Christian religion. And having grown tired of war, he sent a deputation to the great chief of the whites with a present of two hundred oxen, praying him to send him back, in exchange for the cattle, men capable of teaching the blacks. And although this embassy was attacked and his oxen taken, still he sent another messenger to the colony for a man of prayer. Here is the Providence. When Casalis was starting from France, God put it into the heart of this heathen chief to send for a teacher. The messenger of the chief and the messenger of God, Casalis, met at Cape Town. So Casalis with his companions accepted the call and set out on a journey of twelve hundred miles northeast until at last they arrived at Thaba Bosiou, the capital of Basutoland. On the way, Casalis, who had the misfortune to be very near-sighted, had his spectacles ground to pieces in his pocket. He was in consternation. All he could do was to go back and buy others, for the wilds to which he was going would not produce them. So back to the town of Graff Reinet he went, but no spectacles were to be found there; none could be had nearer than Cape Town and it would take three months to get them to him in the wilderness. So he set out again to catch up to his caravan. He was riding along on the high road when suddenly what seemed a lion's head was put over the hedge along the road; at first he thought it was a dog, then he was sure it was a lion. Greatly frightened, he determined to go back, but what surprised him was that his horse did not seem to be frightened. After the first fright was over, as he wiped his brow of the perspiration that the lion had caused, he said to himself, "I have had the honor of exchanging looks with a lion in full daylight and in his own dominions." But his adventures were not over. Soon after he saw six more lions as large as the first. He passed them and to his surprise lived. By evening he had caught up to his company and was seated before a great fire eating his supper. He told them he had seen seven lions which greatly surprised them as they had seen none. The next day as their wagons were rolling on suddenly he saw one of the lions and he grasped another missionary's arm saying, "There are the lions; now you will believe the country is full of them." His companion, roaring with laughter, said: "Those are not lions. They are gnus, a kind of inoffensive antelope, whose head appears at a distance like that of a lion's." His nearsighted eyes had been at fault. How many lions in the way do we imagine we see, which after all are chained like Bunyan's in Pilgrims Progress, or are unreal as in Casalis' case? How many lions in the way have appeared before us in our missionary work but who turned out to be only phantoms?

At Thaba Bosiou they met Moshesh, the most enlightened and upright chief in South Africa, who had sent for them and who lived in a mountain fortress and gladly welcomed them, by placing the whole country at their disposal. But they did not settle on his mountain capital, as they wanted to locate near a stream, so that they might introduce farming. They therefore chose one of the most beautiful valleys twenty miles south of Thaba Bosiou and called it Moriah. Here Casalis found as his best helper Gosselin, who was a practical mechanic. When Gosselin had heard in France that a layman was wanted by the Missionary Society, he cried right out in the meeting: "That means me, I am the man;" and in three days he was ready to go. Mainly through Gosselin's efforts a little hut was erected for the missionaries, and Casalis went back to the Cape to get the furniture and herds for the settlement. On his return occurred an illustration of the dangers that gathered around them. One evening at ten o'clock, as the little company was gathered around the main fire for worship, they heard the convulsive hiccough that a lion makes when about to spring on his prey. Instinctively he started the hymn, the Hottentots, who are great singers, joining in with great earnestness and volume. Their singing must have frightened the lion, for the next day they saw his tracks and realized that God had saved them through a hymn.

Casalis and his companions soon began to give religious instruction, but the work was very slow. The first difficulty was the language, which, as there was no grammar, they had to pick up word by word. They had at first as an interpreter a native who knew a little Dutch, but knew nothing about religion. He had only one word for religion, namely prayer. So when the missionaries urged believing or repenting, he always interpreted it praying. Some of his blunders were even laughable. Thus he confounded the Dutch word Zaligmaker (Saviour) with Zedalmaker (saddle-maker), and so told the Basutos that Jesus was the great saddle-maker. His whole manner left the impression that he did not believe a word that he was translating. He suggested to the missionaries that the best way to convert the Basutos was to thrash them well. And he went so far as to offer his services, saying: "I will help you, and you will see how well I can handle the whip." By and by as the missionaries learned more of the language, they detected his tricks and soon sent him off.

The missionaries began their religious services by reciting stories from the Bible, and finally composed several hymns. This captivated the Basutos, for singing was a new art to them, and they joined in it with great gusto. The only difficulty the missionaries had was in keeping them from beating time with their feet with all their might, and thus making more noise than music. However a more serious difficulty arose when the missionaries began prayer. For as long as the natives saw that the missionary was speaking to them, they would keep quiet; but when he was no longer speaking to them, they felt under no obligation to listen. Some would look one way and others another. Some would gape and others begin talking. At length the missionaries hit on the plan of having them say the petitions after them. This the natives liked, as they were fond of hearing their own voices.

Casalis and his companions having started this little settlement, determined that they would make another visit to Thaba Bosiou to the chief. "Now," he said, "you will indeed be my missionary. Every time you come, I will be there to get my people to listen to you." The king kept his word. Every time the missionary arrived, the public crier mounted the platform near the king's house, where the gatherings of the tribe were held, and cried with all his power: "To prayer, everybody, women and children as well." This command caused great commotion and merriment at first; for an audience to which women were admitted was unknown. Especially the young men watched to see what the matrons and maidens would do. The women first sent their children, hoping that would suffice. But Moshesh was inexorable. "The women, where are they?" he asked. Finally they came; dazed, yet curious. But they stayed at the entrance of the enclosure as far from the speaker as possible, where they squatted and squeezed together like a flock of sheep, taking care to turn their backs to the meeting. The missionaries thus found not only a field of labor, but also a church building (of its kind) at their disposal, and a chief to aid them by his example and influence.

The conversations between the missionary and the chief are among the most interesting things which M. Casalis has placed on record, and gives us a pleasing expression of the intellectual strength, penetration, simplicity and candor of this remarkable man. We quote two instances which remind us of Paul's description of some among the heathen in his days, as "feeling after God if happily they might find him."

"You believe then," said the king one evening to the missionary, pointing to the stars, "that in the midst and beyond all these there is an all-powerful Master, who has created all, and is our Father? Our ancestors used, in fact, to speak of a Lord of Heaven, and we still call these great shining spots (the Milky Way), you see above you, the way of the gods; but it seemed to us that the world must have existed forever, except, however, men and animals, who, according to us, have had a beginning —animals having come first and men afterwards.

But we did not know who gave them existence. We adored the spirits of our ancestors, and we asked of them rain, abundant harvests, good health, and a good reception amongst them after death."

"You were in darkness," was the answer, "and we have brought you the light. All these visible things, and a multitude of others which we cannot see, have been created and are preserved by a Being, all-wise and all-good, who is God of us all, and who has made us to be born of one blood."

Moshesh was greatly struck when he heard the missionaries enumerate the commandments of the Decalogue. "That," said he, "is written in all our hearts. We did not know the God you announced to us, and we had no idea of the Sabbath; but in all the rest of your law we find nothing new. We knew it was very wicked to be ungrateful and disobedient to parents, to rob, to kill, to commit adultery, to covet the property of another, and to bear false witness."

For five years the missionaries labored at Moriah without gaining a convert. The Basutos were friendly, but not willing to take the decisive step. But on the evening of January 9, 1836, they heard a sound near their hut at Moriah. Going out they discovered one of their young men, Sekhesa, praying. As they listened to the young man's prayer of consecration, they fell on their knees and burst into tears of joy at his conversion. Sekhesa remained faithful till his death in 1881. Some weeks after his first prayer Arbousset read a hymn on the second coming of Christ. The poor negro with beaming countenance ejaculated: "Blessed be His name." Hundreds of Basutos afterward acknowledged that their first religious impressions came to them at the time when Sekhesa asked the Lord to make him His child.

The missionaries finally decided that so important a point as Thaba Bosiou, the capital, ought not to be without a missionary. So Casalis was appointed to locate there. He did not, however, set up his house on the top of the hill on which the town was built, but at its base; so that he might farm the land around his hut. Becoming lonely, he set out for Cape Town in search of a wife. When he arrived there, he felt very awkward, for he had been so long in the wilderness that he had forgotten what civilization was, and felt like fleeing and hiding himself.

When Casalis returned to his first station, Moriah,

he found that the presence of his wife created quite a sensation. The Basutos had never seen a white woman before. At first they hesitated somewhat to come near, but soon curiosity got the better of them, and they approached her. They indulged in all manner of remarks about her. They analyzed her features—admired specially the smallness of her mouth and the whiteness of her skin. Every act of hers was noted. When she ate, they said she eats like a bird. They were very much surprised that she did not go out with her husband into the field and dig as they did. But they thus learned that Christians cared for their wives, and did not make slaves of them as the heathen did. The effect of this marriage was that the female part of the population at once recognized in her a missionary to themselves, and came to her with their troubles and cares. They began to flock to church. For since Casalis' wife went to church, it was clear to them that a woman had a soul to save.

Casalis and his wife then went to Thaba Bosiou, June, 1838. The appearance of Mrs. Casalis at the capital created the same sensation that it had done at Moriah. The church service began to be more largely attended, increasing from two hundred to four hundred. A Sabbath at Thaba Bosiou was a very interesting day. At ten in the morning Moshesh, the chief, would come down from his mountain capital with his followers to service. As it would have been wearisome to go up the steep mountain and return again to the second service, they remained on the plain, spending the day around the missionaries' house. The men and women, old and young, tried to read the spelling book and the little catechism. At first they protested that the black man never could make paper speak. Moshesh's father was a superstitious old heathen, and ridiculed the fact that they could learn to read. "Lies, lies," he said. "I will never believe that a word can become visible." One day there was a tremendous discovery made by ten or twelve of them. They suddenly discovered that they could, without any help, make out the meaning of several phrases they had never read before. And Moshesh's skeptical father was stupefied with wonder. When once the Basutos had begun to learn to read, the knowledge of the Bible spread rapidly. During the revival that followed in all the mission stations, twenty-seven converts were baptized, and forty-two other adults soon followed them.

A most significant conversion was that of Libe, the uncle of Moshesh. When the missionaries first came, although he was a man of eighty, and hovering over the grave, he urged that they be driven away. Indeed he left Thaba Bosiou partly because he wanted to get away from the influence of the missionaries. But, although he forsook them, they did not forsake him. When they visited him, he said: "Depart from me, I will have nothing to do with you and your God." Sometime after that, when Casalis was officiating at the funeral of one of Libe's daughters (whose husband happened to be a Christain), Libe rushed at Casalis in rage. Casalis expected nothing else but that he would have to defend himself. Fortunately Libe's sons rushed to him, imploring him to stop. Libe refused. And his own children were under the sad necessity of forcing him to the ground and holding him there during the entire service. Finally when Casalis again passed him, Libe, in his rage and helplessness, knocked his head on the ground again and again. But God can save to the uttermost. And one day, after the missionaries had discontinued their visits, because they felt that they only angered him, they were surprised to receive an invitation to go and see him.

The messenger who brought it said, with his face radiant with joy: "Libe prays. Yesterday Libe sent to my hut and asked: 'Can you pray? Kneel down with me and pray God to have mercy on the greatest of sinners. Who will deliver me from the fire that will never be quenched? Do you think God will pardon me? I refused to go and hear His word when still able to walk. Now I am blind and almost deaf; how can I serve Jehovah?'" "Here," said the messenger, Libe stopped and asked me, "have you your book (the Bible) with you?" The messenger said he had. "Well," said Libe, "open it and place my finger on the name of God. The messenger said he had done so. "It is there," cried Libe, "the beautiful name of God. Now place my finger on that of Jesus, my Saviour." Casalis having heard this from the messenger, hastened to Libe. He found him penitent. And as Casalis repeated his visits, grace made him as docile as a little child. In his anxiety to be saved, Libe generally took Casalis' hands in his, and putting his ear close to Casalis' lips, repeated the words Casalis uttered, begging him meanwhile to correct him, if in his deafness he made a mistake. A more touching sight can hardly be imagined than this blind, deaf heathen thus repenting of his past sins, and seeking Christ and heaven. How Libe's anxiety to be saved rebukes many careless ones in this Christian land. Libe's baptism attracted a large crowd. Five aged members of the church carried him on a couch, for he was too feeble to move alone. Very soon after his baptism he died. His grandson asked him whether he knew it was the Lord's day. He replied, "I know it. I am with my Lord." And in a few moments he fell asleep, to be with his Lord forever.

But the most important conversion in the mission was that of Moshesh, the chief. He was a most remarkable, far-seeing man—"the most original, able and upright barbarous chief South Africa has ever had," says Orpen, a British magistrate. The greatness of his character is shown by an illustration. In 1852 he was attacked by the British. Compelled to defend themselves, the Basutos drove the British back. They planned a night attack when the worn-out British soldiers would probably have been overcome, but suddenly an order came from Moshesh stopping the fight. The next morning Moshesh sent a messenger to the English commander (Would any conqueror of Europe have treated an enemy so?) saying: "Oh, my master, I am still your man, I am still a child of the Queen. Sometimes a man beats a dog and the dog puts his teeth in his hand and gives him a bite, nevertheless, the dog loves the master and the master loves the dog and will not kill it. I am ashamed of what happened yesterday. Let it be forgotten." The British could not refuse such magnanimity. They at once made peace, but how noble was Moshesh in being the first to ask for peace.

Moshesh welcomed the missionaries from the very beginning, and would come, Nicodemus-like, to visit Casalis by night and talk about this new religion. But, like Nicodemus, he postponed decision. He however paid great attention to the preaching, and would often repeat the whole sermon and explain it point by point to the people who did not understand it. But year after year he postponed decision. In 1869, as he was getting old, Casalis went to him and urged him to prepare for the judgment. He wept and prayed, but like so many, could not make up his mind. However in 1870, after thirty-seven years of prayer by the missionaries, a messenger called the missionaries to him, for he was ready. His description of his conversion was given in a very simple-hearted way, just as the heathen would express themselves. Seeing one of the missionaries, he said to him, "How old is your baby?" "Three months," replied the missionary. "Then," said the chief, referring to his new-birth, "he is just my age. I have only just been born. It is only now that I begin to be a man." He asked to be allowed to see this child. His eyes filled with tears, as he said: "My child, you are my thaka (one of the same age); you have shown me the way I shall get to Jesus."

The day before his death he sent the missionaries the message: "Tell them they will be too late." And so it was, for he was to have been baptized on Sunday, but died on Friday. His last instructions were: "Let the missionaries not be weary to teach my people, and especially my sons." His mind seemed to go again to his thaka (the missionary's child), as he said: "Kiss also that child, Thaka Moshesh. May he grow up to be a great blessing to my people." He died with the filial cry: "Let me go to my Father; I am already very near Him. Hold me up that I may fly," and his spirit went up to its God. Thus died in Christian hope the noblest chieftain in South Africa.

What trophies of redeeming grace have been won there for Christ! The hope is that through the

French missionaries, the rich temperament and capacity which distinguishes the Basutos may cause them to be an influential factor in making the Dark Continent gain light under the rays of the Sun of Righteousness.

Casalis, to the sorrow of the mission, was recalled to France in 1856, where he became director of the Paris Missionary Society, and head of its training institute for missionaries. He lived at Paris for many years, enthusing the home church, and by his knowledge of the foreign field, aiding the Board of the Mission Society. The French government finally came to see the greatness of his work and honored him with the title of "Knight of the Legion of Honor." He died in 1893.*

---

*"My Life in Basutoland," by Casalis, published by the Religious Tract Society, London, ought to be in all our Sunday-school libraries.

Chapter III.
ADOLPH MABILLE.

Another great missionary of the French Reformed Church in Africa was the Rev. Adolph Mabille. He was the heart and centre of a great work which Robert Moffat pronounced the most successful of all missions.

He was born June 12, 1836, at Baulmes, near Yverdon, in the canton of Vaud, Switzerland. He was a precocious boy. Educated at Yverdon and later at Basle, he was ready to enter the Theological School at Lausanne before he was old enough to be admitted. He therefore traveled in Holland and England, and in 1854 accepted the position of teacher of French in a Quaker school at Kendal, England. It was while there that his religious experience was greatly deepened and that the missionary call came to him. One day an agent of the British Bible Society arrived at Kendal, who made his acquaintance. Seeing the rich promise in the young man he approached him on the subject of missions. Striking him on the shoulder, he asked him the simple but pointed question: "Young man, have you ever thought of the millions of Chinese who die without a knowledge of the Saviour?" The question went to his heart like an arrow. He said: "Behold! I come, Lord, to do Thy will."

He applied to the Paris Missionary Society and entered their mission house at Paris to prepare himself for foreign mission work under the care of Casalis. His desire was to go to China, to which his attention had been called. His thoughts and prayers were continually for that country. The committee of the Missionary Society was at that time disposed to send missionaries to China, and Mabille would have been sent, being well fitted by his ability and experience in teaching. But as he heard Casalis speak so often and lovingly of his Basutos, and fell in love with Adele, the daughter of Casalis whom he afterwards married, his mind was turned to Africa. They were married May 17, 1859. On the third of July, 1859, amid the salvos of artillery which announced in Paris the victory of the French over the Austrians at Solferino, he and another missionary, Germond, were ordained in the Church of the Oratoire at Paris. The young missionary couple afterwards visited Yverdon and Geneva. At Geneva his visit led to the formation of a missionary society which aided him to found his

Bible school for the training of evangelists, at Moriah, in South Africa.

Together with Mr. and Mrs. Germond they sailed from England in July, 1859, and landed at Cape Town October 30, where he was met by Rev. Mr. Bisseaux. After resting, they started forward on their long journey to their mission station, Betheulia, where they arrived January 12, 1860. One of his first impressions was that of astonishment that the missionaries had not yet translated or printed the Bible in the language of the Basutos. He at once set himself about doing so. He did not understand the language, but Dyke dictated to him and he wrote it down. They began with the book of Joshua. He afterward made a tour of the various stations of the mission. He attended in April the Synod of the mission and was then appointed as missionary to Moriah, the oldest station. He and his wife arrived there June 7, 1860. The station had been greatly devastated by the Boers in the war of 1858. The parsonage had been burned and he had to suffer great inconvenience. Besides, the membership of the mission had become scattered. His progress in their language had by this time become so great that on the Sunday after his installation he attempted to preach and succeeded fairly well, his great linguistic powers aiding him.

His marriage with the daughter of the former missionary, Casalis, gave him great influence over the Basutos who loved her for her father's sake. They used to say of her: "She is our mother. She was born in our land, and she is one of us, and what she says is good." She was worthy of this confidence; for she was a remarkable woman. He founded a normal school at Moriah to train teachers. While its organization was being considered, who should arrive at the mission but the Rev. Alexander Duff, the great Scotch missionary to India, and the originator of the system of educational missions, to counsel them. This school was originally begun in time of war. As he came back to look after his people at Moriah he was detained there, and while the war cloud hung heavily around them he gathered a few young men and taught them to teach others. He had twenty students at first. From this normal school a system of schools spread all through the Basuto tribe.

But he was a pastor as well as a teacher. He had twenty stations in connection with his mission at Moriah. Twice a year their members came to

Moriah for the Lord's Supper. These were scenes never to be forgotten, when hundreds of the Lord's followers gathered on the green hillside under the shadow of the great mountains around and surrounded the Lord's table to show forth his death till he come. His membership arose from 234 in 1861 to 1692 in 1894. His scholars arose from 160 in 1860 to 1306 in 1890, and 906 in 1894. He also installed a press at Moriah. In 1880 he re-visited France, so as to publish the Bible in their language, and returned with a new printing press. On it he published a number of books, as the Chants of Zion, a book of sacred song, for he was a fine musician and splendid singer. He also published a pastoral theology, Sessouto Dictionary, a Biblical Dictionary and other books. This printing press was important because by it 250,000 of the Basutos were reached. A Bible for the Basutos was finally published in 1882 as the result of his work.

The normal school grew into a school of evangelists in 1876. The first student soon grew into five students. In two years he had twenty. Many of them were from other districts in South Africa, as the Transvaal. Thus in 1878 ten were from the Transvaal and two from Orange Free State, five belonged to the Dutch Reformed Church,* four to the Swiss mission and one to the Berlin mission—more strangers than from the Basutos. This showed the popularity of his school and the excellence of its course of study. His labors were incessant, as he began teaching at 6 a. m. He thoroughly believed in educational missions. He said: "Our native Christians can help their own people better than we missionaries can."

He was also an explorer in regions beyond, opening up the district afterwards taken by the French Reformed Mission of Switzerland. He prepared for the later mission of Coillard to the Zambesi in the north. Together with Coillard he went to Europe and pled for the opening of a new mission on the Zambesi. His parish would frequently be swept with wave after wave of God's Spirit, when he dealt very wisely with those under conviction of sin, and led them to Christ. He was very earnest in his piety, becoming somewhat inclined to the higher life theory. The visit of Major Malan strengthened this in him for a time. And he went with Coillard to King Williamstown in Cape Colony

---

*The Boers have not been considered favorable to missions, but this church has had a successful mission at Zoutpantburg, for many years, Rev. S. Hofmeyer being the missionary.

in 1875, to attend sanctification meetings for total deliverance from sin. The writings of Rev. Andrew Murray, the Nestor of the Dutch Reformed Church of South Africa, strengthened him in these mild perfectionist views.

In secular affairs he was much tried. The missionaries of the Paris Society were placed in very difficult positions often, because, though French, they labored in British territory. They, therefore, tried to avoid all political complications, but occasionally they were compelled to take part in them, although they did so with great reluctance. Owing to his close proximity to the chief, Letsie, Mabille was forced to occupy himself somewhat with secular affairs. He and his colleagues took an honorable part in the establishment of the British protectorate over the Basutos, which saved them from entire destruction at the hands of the Boers. But during the war of 1880-1881 the Cape government decided that it was wise to make all the blacks give up their arms into the hands of the British government. This act would have left the Basutos utterly defenseless and at the mercy of hostile whites. Mabille openly took sides against this order in the interest of the mission. He wrote about it to a leading citizen of Cape Colony, to the prime minister, to the governor. Had his counsel been followed the colony would have been saved a war and the cost of at least $15,000,000. But while he took this ground in writing to the English, among the Basutos he preached peace, condemning the recourse to arms as unjustifiable. Providentially he was in Europe when the war broke out. His efforts led him to be severely criticized, but also gained him the greatest popularity among the Basutos.

In all this he reveals his intense activity. One of his fellow missionaries said of him: "It is no use to relieve Mabille in his work, for as soon as he is relieved in one thing he finds something else to do." His severe labors finally broke down his health. His work as pastor, teacher, preacher, publisher, explorer, proved too much for him. Still he kept on. The Paris Society wanted one of its missionaries to go with Coillard to Bechuanaland; Mabille and his wife went. At first he seemed benefited by this journey. He attended the Basuto conference in April, 1894, though he only when lying on a couch could be present at the meetings. Then he went to Leribe where his son was stationed as evangelist. He returned to Moriah May 10. Although in great pain, he proceeded with the examination of candidates for admission to his Bible school.

On May 15 a physician arrived and examined him, saying: "It is grave, very grave." Mabille expressed a great desire to live so that he might revise the Basuto Bible. He had just finished an English-Basuto Dictionary, the work of 20 years. When they hesitated to tell him his condition he insisted. When told, he prayed long. Then he said: "Lord, O place my work low; I have endeavored to labor, but how many times I have transgressed. But I shall not want, thou knowest it." On May 17 he bade farewell to his friends. On the 19th he admitted to his dying bed the chief of the Lessouto, to whom he addressed pressing appeals for his conversion and for temperance.

Sunday, May 20, 1894, was a glorious day, full of the very atmosphere of heaven. The early hours of the day he spent in praying for each of his catechists, schoolmasters, elders in his district, about 150 in number, and for the students of the Bible school, who were that day at religious work. When those about him wondered that he could remember names so well he said: "O, you know I have prayed for them so often by name." When he heard the church bells ring, he exclaimed: "Glory, glory in the highest heaven!" and then said: "Jesus, I am also one of the worshippers." A young man wanted to see him. "Yes," he said, "let him in. I have a lovely message for him." After talking earnestly with him, he said: "I wish I could impress on your heart the invitation that Christ is your Saviour." Afterwards he clapped his hands joyfully, exclaiming: "Bravo! they are going to reach the Zambezi," showing that his thoughts were with Coillard and his distant mission. At 7.30 p. m. he passed to rest. "At eventide it shall be light,"—his labors of thirty-four years were over, and he had gone to his reward.

His funeral was very large. Everywhere it was felt: "Knowest thou not that a great man has fallen in Israel?" In the cemetery at Moriah is a plain stone with a marble slab on which are the words: "Adolph Mabille, 1836-94." His blessing remained in his family. All of the children became Christians and two of the sons and two of the daughters became missionaries. But the larger blessing remained with the mission, whose success was so largely due to the foundations he laid.

Before leaving this splendid mission of the Paris Society among the Basutos we will briefly describe their work. A most fortunate circumstance for the mission was the fact that there were no wars in Basutoland for fifteen years up to 1848. This period of peace was very favorable to the mission. The year 1848 was, however, a very trying one. On account of the revolution in France, the Mission Society became so impoverished that it had to close its mission house at Paris, and the missionaries began to suffer. But in its need, friends in the colony in Africa who had seen its glorious work, nobly came to its relief. Indeed, money was sent unexpectedly from distant lands, as Holland and India, to help them tide over their difficulties, the whole amount being $10,000. The next year Casalis went back to France and stirred the churches most wonderfully with his tales of South Africa and of the wonders of mission work. Meanwhile bitter wars were carried on between the Boers and the English in South Africa. The British, by giving up Basutoland in 1855, left it at the mercy of the Boers. In two of the wars Moshesh, the Basuto chief, lost part of his territory, so that four of the mission stations had to be given up. And yet there was a blessing in it all. How often afflictions are blessings. As in Madagascar, so in Basutoland; when the missionaries were driven out and war and famine prevailed, then the Church was revived. The season from 1865 to 1868 was a time of wonderful revival. The result was that by the end of the war all the congregations were largely increased.

During that war the Christians of Moriah, like those referred to in the eleventh chapter of Hebrews fled to the caves and dens in the mountain above their home. There, for three years, more than 300 Christians were preserved. Morning and evening they prayed and sang praises. Their enemies heard them, but no cannon ball could reach them. Philemon, the schoolmaster of Moriah, was raised up of God to be their pastor in the caves. For three years he watched over this large congregation, numbering about 800 souls. As they had not much to do, much time was spent in preaching and prayer. At the close of the war Philemon brought 100 converts for baptism. In all there were 436 candidates for admission at Moriah after the war. Philemon was a true apostle, putting many lazy Christians in Christian lands to shame. After the war, famine and then typhus fever came. Philemon was devoted in attending to the sick, until he finally caught the disease. His dying was beautiful.

He was asked whether he would like to go to his Lord. He replied: "Yes, very much." When asked if he would like to remain and work for the Lord, he replied: "Yes, very much." Living or dying, he wished to be the Lord's. And just before he breathed his last, what did he do but give a sign for the whistle, with which for three years he had called the churches in the dens to prayer and praise. He put it to his mouth and tried to sound it once more before he died. A faithful watchman he was to the very last.

The results of this mission have been most gratifying. From a temporal point of view the arrival of the missionaries proved to be the salvation of the Basutos. The country in 1813 was almost uninhabited, but it is now covered with hamlets surrounded by fields in a high state of cultivation. Had the Basutos remained heathen, they would have been cut off by the wars or have killed each other off. Now they have peace and civilization. But the results spiritually have been even greater. Although the wars compelled the society to give up five stations, and to centre their efforts on Basutoland, they still have thirteen principal stations and 129 out-stations, with day schools scattered all through the country, having 8,000 children in them. In 1888, out of a population of 200,000, 25,000 were adherents of the mission and 35,000 were under Christian influences. At present there are 12,676 communicants, and 11,626 pupils in the schools. Their worship is the same as in the French Protestant Churches, which are prevailingly Reformed.

This Paris Society also opened other mission stations. When the French gained the Society Islands in the South Pacific, where the London Missionary Society had had a successful mission, the latter turned its mission over to the Paris Society, and there are now about 4,000 members and 1,800 scholars. And in 1887 the American Presbyterian mission turned over its missions on the Gaboon and Ogove rivers to them, because they were in French territory. Still the Basuto mission has always remained the most important. Many are its trophies. One was Makoniane, Moshesh's Marshal Ney. He who planned the Basuto empire now sits at the feet of Jesus, confessing Him. But the most important was the conversion of Moshesh, the Basuto chief, over whose tomb should be inscribed: "Thy gentleness made thee great." The society has pushed out northward on the Zambesi where, after years of discouragement, they gained their first convert in

1892, and now the king Lewanika begins to show interest in Christianity.

The importance of the work done by this French mission cannot be over-estimated. Why was the Gospel more successful among the Basutos than among the Zulu tribes of South Africa? Because, as Malan says, the Gospel was preached to them before the white man had entered their territory even for trade. But it was preached to the Zulus after they had been at war with the Dutch settlers. The Basutos knew nothing of the evils accompanying European occupation. The chief of the Basutos did everything to encourage the Gospel but the chief of the Zulus did everything for a long time to hinder it. Another reason for its spread was the fact that the Basutos are a gentle race compared with the Zulus.

For they have evangelized the most hopeful of the South African tribes, the Basutos, whose rich capacity for improvement will make them a power for evangelizing the dark continent. France is now one of the largest land-owners in Africa, especially in the north, although she has possessions in the south. In view of this, the importance of the French mission becomes much greater. She is the crown jewel in the old Huguenot Church.

Yours cordially, F. Coillard

Chapter IV.

FRANCIS AND CHRISTINA COILLARD

The greatest living missionary of the French Reformed Church is Francis Coillard. He was born July 17, 1834, at Asnieres des Bourges, France. After suffering various hardships in his early life, he at last attained his long desire to be a missionary and was admitted to the Mission House at Paris. After pursuing the usual course there he was ordained May 24, 1857. After laboring in the Basuto mission for several years, he was married in 1861 to Miss Christina McIntosh. As she is one of the most distinguished missionary heroines of the nineteenth century, we will pause on her life.

She was the daughter of a Scotch clergyman, having been born at Greenock, Scotland, November 29, 1829. When a girl she had great love for missions, as she had subscribed out of her pocket money to a missionary paper, and her heart beat with indignation at seeing Sarah Roby, a poor child who had been buried alive by her heathen parents, but fortunately rescued by a missionary and who was taken all over the British Isles as a proof of the pagan horrors. In 1855 Miss McIntosh gave lessons in Paris, where she met Mr. Coillard while studying at the Mission House. Four years after his departure for Africa she followed him thither. She was a spiritually minded woman and a great aid to her husband. "Never," she said, "never will you find me between you and duty. Wherever you have to go, be it to the end of the world, I shall follow you." How wonderfully and nobly she carried this out.

At first they were located at Leribe among the Basutos where, after a year's work, they rejoiced over two converts. But their work had its difficulties. One of the chiefs, Molapo, the son of Moshesh the king, had backslidden from Christianity and greatly oppressed the Christians. Yet Coillard would talk to him faithfully about his soul. Even when living in sin (for he became a polygamist), it is said he never would retire at night without reading his Bible and praying. At times his spiritual struggles were so great as to almost destroy his reason, when he would flee to the mountains and hide in a cave.

One day Coillard tried to rouse his memory by asking: "Tell me, what did you feel when you were converted." "My pastor," he said, "it was not an illusion of the imagination. There was a fire that devoured me. I could not hold it in; but now," he added in a tone of bitter sadness, "it has all gone out—there is nothing left but a heap of ashes." He died as he had lived—away from God, although his last act at dying was to ask that the missionaries be sent for. But they came too late.

War also came and devastated their district. In 1865 he was driven out by the Boer war. So hasty was their departure that Mrs. Coillard did not have time to take the bread that she was baking out of the oven. Their church bell, packed carelessly in a wagon in their haste, sounded a funeral knell all along the road. They were told they would never be allowed to return, but they did return after the three years' war was over. They then found their church building in ruins. But most remarkable, they found that the congregation had grown in their absence and in spite of the war to fifty, due to the evangelist who remained. Their membership continued to grow so that when in 1876 the Basuto synod met at Leribe, the attendance was so great that some of them had to sleep in the caves of the surrounding mountains.

But Providence was preparing Coillard for a

greater mission than among the Basutos. The Basutos learned that a large tribe up the Zambezi river speaking their language was destitute of the Gospel. They determined to send it to them. In 1874 one of the evangelists, Asher, was ordered to visit the Banyai tribe farther north. He came back with a most eloquent plea for missionaries for them. He said: "Ah, why could I not cut off my arms and legs and make every limb of mine a missionary to the Banyai?" He reported that three of the chiefs had already offered sites for mission stations.

His address was electric in its effect. At one memorial meeting an old man rose and said, "We've had enough of talking. Let us do something," and going to the communion table he laid upon it half a crown. The whole congregation followed his example and the movement spread to other stations. After the custom of the French churches to give some offering on Communion Sunday, they came one communion day,—men, women and children, and even babes at their mother's breasts, were gathered at the sacred table to lay upon it their offerings for this new mission. In a short time $2,500 was raised, not counting, cattle large and small, that were offered. The Missionary Conference could no longer hesitate. They chose four men to go. This was a beautiful illustration of converted heathen sending the Gospel to convert the heathen.

It happened that just at that time Major Malan, a grandson of the famous Rev. Cæsar Malan, of Geneva, who had resigned his commission in the British army to do soldier work for the Captain of our salvation, visited these French missions of South Africa. This visit led to a wonderful spiritual uplift in the mission. One day in crossing the river Kei, when they had climbed up its slope, overcome with an irresistible impulse, Malan says: "We all sprang from our horses, knelt in the shadow of the bush—I still see it before me—then taking ourselves as witnesses we offered ourselves individually to the new mission, an act of deep solemnity which made us all brothers in arms." Immediately we remounted, Major Malan spurred his horse, galloped up the hill, and called out: "Three soldiers ready to conquer Africa." This was the true beginning of the Barotsi mission on the Zambesi.

A newly arrived missionary, Dieterlen, was sent to the new field in 1875, only to be arrested and imprisoned by the Boers and the expedition broken up. But Coillard rose above the danger. "Even if their missionary had been imprisoned," he said, "the Gospel entered Europe by a prison. Forward! Forward!" As a result just at the time when he and his wife were preparing to take a much needed rest in France, after ten years' absence, the missionary conference asked him to go on an exploring expedition to the Banyai. Hard as it was to give up their long-cherished plans, they started April, 1877, accompanied by several native evangelists. They soon found themselves in most perilous situations. Soon after they came to a border chief of the Banyai named Masonda. At his invitation they visited his capital where they found themselves surrounded by threatening blacks and unable to escape. A plot was laid to kill them. Coillard and his wife were being led by some of these natives, one of them taking Mrs. Coillard's arm, along slippery rocks, when one of the evangelists said, "Where are they leading our mother?" Coillard looked up and saw before them an abyss. He seized his wife and tore her from the hands of the savages and then succeeded in making their way back to the camp. But they learned later that the chief had planned to throw them all over the precipice. With great difficulty, though surrounded by armed savages for several days, they at last succeeded in escaping from this chief. At one time as the savages pressed so closely on the caravan, Coillard could, with difficulty, prevent his company from shooting, which would only have resulted in a massacre of them all. At another time another chief, Chibi, would have murdered him, if his faithful evangelist had not thrown himself between Coillard and the knife.

A few weeks after leaving the treacherous Masonda, they were seized by an armed caravan and carried to Lobengula, the king of the Matabele tribe, who kept them prisoners for four months. He treated them with kindness, but was angered that they had entered his territory without his knowledge. He finally refused to allow them to settle in his land, and sent them out of it. Thus their mission to the Banyai had been refused. Discouraged and driven out, they went to the Barotsi tribe who spoke the same language as the Basutos. There they were gladly received by the border-clans of the tribe. Livingston had been among them and had left the name of missionary in good odor. Coillard said he felt not a little humiliated at being continually called by them "Doctor," as they had done to Livingston. He says: "Thus it is that the first missionary that comes along is invested with the boots of this giant."

At Shesheke he evangelized with success among them as he could speak their language and they were quite receptive to the Gospel. But one after another his evangelists died. "Their tombs," he said, "shall be the finger-posts to point the way for the new missions." While staying there Major Serpo Pinto, the Portuguese explorer, sent by Portugal to offset the increasing power of England in Africa, came to them in utter destitution and sick with the fever. Mrs. Coillard nursed him to health and the explorer pays a fine tribute to them and their work in his book. During this expedition the caravan was attacked by lions. Water was scarce, and Mr. Coillard suffered much from fever, and both himself and his wife were greatly worn out when they at last returned to the Basutos. They had reached in two years the Barotsi tribe on the Upper Zambesi river, a journey of 1,000 miles through the dense, wild wilderness. He had penetrated as far as the north bank of the Zambesi, but the rainy season prevented further progress, although

MADAME C. COILLARD.

the king of the Barotsi had invited them. Considering her sex, Mrs. Coillard's journey was as great as any of Stanley's in Africa.

But although their journey seemed fruitless, yet it gave the inspiration for the founding of a new mission. They brought the news to the Basutos that away up north, on the north side of the Zambesi river, was a tribe that spoke their language. Were they not therefore responsible to carry the gospel to them, especially as they had so cordially received the missionaries? But the Reformed Church of France was at that time too weak to undertake the great work of founding a new mission. For this reason Coillard did what he had hoped to do two years before. He and his wife went home to France January, 1880, after an absence of 22 years, having labored at Leribe 20 years. They spent two years in Europe travelling everywhere in the interest of the new mission. With great eloquence, but with great humbleness, he plead for this new work. The fragility of his body, which the Zambesi fever had almost burned up, gave increased power to his words. He traveled through France, Switzerland, Holland, Belgium, everywhere, at mission meetings and conferences, presenting his cause. His wife was also indefatigable in aiding him, and merited more than ever the beautiful pronoun "we," which he was wont to use of her in his letters.

In August, 1882, they returned to Leribe in Africa, alas, to find the church devastated and scattered by war. Six months were required to bring order out of chaos.

Finally on January 2, 1884, they started for the new field on the Zambesi, with six wagons drawn by oxen. What faith it required to make so long a journey into the wilderness! There were wild beasts to be feared and sickness far from help, and wilder men, worse than beasts. Though near the tropics it became so cold at night that one of them said humorously: "There aren't any tropics; I don't believe in them," as he muffled himself in his cloak. And Coillard says: "Every one laughed and that warmed them up." He found that the Jesuits had already established themselves in that country, but in the providence of God they were soon compelled to leave. The farther he traveled, the darker, morally, Africa seemed. He says: "A historian speaking of George IV. has said that if he had been stripped of all his waistcoats in which he had a mania for muffling himself, you might have searched in vain for a man. I can say the same of the Zambesians. I believe that under the pile of all that is hideous in paganism we shall find men, and men whom we can love."

By October 17 he had come to Leshoma, south of the Zambesi, where Mrs. Coillard remained while he went ahead to explore. His photographs created quite an excitement. He had to show them his sun (his watch), and then a mirror, which the young women never forget. He says: "An old woman, who could not believe that his whole body was as white as his face, on seeing his bare arm, cried out in a tone of compassion that quite touched me: 'It is possible! He is like a new born child.'"

He appeared before the court at Lealuyi and was cordially welcomed, though the prime minister, Gambella, said: "We have yellow hearts (of envy), and our country is full of blood," which indeed proved only too true. Because Coillard and his evangelist, Aaron, spoke the Sessuto language, the language of the Basutos and also of this tribe, it gave them great popularity. He returned to Leshoma where his wife had meanwhile, in the face of sickness labored hard in forming a school. He said of her: "Are there many women who would thus deprive themselves of the aid and advice of their husbands in such isolations and under such burdens of responsibilities?"

On August 14, 1885, the party left Leshoma and crossed the Zambesi to Shesheke where they arrived December 12, after a journey of 1,000 miles from Basutoland. There for a time they established their mission. Coillard then started for the capital, Lealuyi, where he held the first service.

The king Lewanika, received him kindly, but began to reveal his selfish nature. The king said he wanted to ask him for all sorts of things—candles, coffee, medicine. Coillard replied that he was not a trader. The king said: "And if I want shirts, a hat and shoes, you will have to get them for me." Coillard replied that he could not. And the king was very much astonished, for all the white men he had seen before were traders and he had fleeced them at his pleasure. The king, however, permitted him to hold service in his capital and attended it. Coillard then went back and brought his wife and caravan, January 10, 1887, to Sefula, 300 miles further, in the heart of the Barotsi country and not very far from Lealuyi, where he permanently located the mission. When they arrived there was great excitement at Sefula. Men wrapped in long strips of calico bound round the waist by bands of serpent skins and with white and down rabbit tails in their hair, women in still larger numbers, with their short petticoats of antelope hides and copper and ivory bracelets dangling on their wrists and knees, all were hastening to see that extraordinary phenomenon—a white lady. The air resounded with clapping of hands and shouts of " Hail, hail, lord, good day, O our mother!"

At the end of a ten years' wandering he at last founded his new mission. He at once began services in the open air which he thus describes: "Yesterday (February 27), we had 150 auditors. But it is difficult in the open air to hold these restless spirits captive. It may be the wind, the rain or the sun. It may be a bird flying past, a fowl cackling, or dogs barking or fighting. The people greet each other during the service, they chat, laugh, take snuff, come and go. Still, sometimes they listen. Yesterday I riveted their attention by the story of the deluge, and closed by describing the deluge of fire, prophesied by Peter, and appealed to the audience: "Where will you flee from the wrath of God?" Some of them good-naturedly called out to him, "To thee, O missionary, our father."

They opened a school March 4, holding it under the trees, the lessons in writing being given on the sand. It began with 20 scholars, the king sending two of his sons and five of his nephews. The pupils lived at the expense of the public, and Coillard had stolen by them some of his valuable barometers as well as his poultry and sheep. But he had to bear it without complaint. Finally the school broke up (February, 1888), because the novelty was over and the boys had to go on fighting expeditions. He was, however, surprised to learn that the king, heathen that he was, ordered Sunday to be observed while on these expeditions, for the king had been a regular attendant at his services. But, sad to say, the king, in order to do this, had forced away from Coillard two of his best young men who were inquirers after religion, but who then fell away from him under the king's influence. The king made these two teach him to read and even made them hold public services by praying, singing and preaching. Yet their immoral life made it only a scandal. On November 14, 1887, Coillard had begun his class of catechumens, two in number, one a boy of great promise, Nguana-Ngombe, whom he found praying in the thickets, and asking: "What must I do to be saved?" He later became the first baptized convert, May 25, 1890.

In October, 1888, the school began again with 48 pupils of whom Litia, the king's son, was the leader. Coillard also approached the king on his return from his expeditions: "When will you become a believer?" "When I know how to read," was his reply. "Why should you wait? Has not your conscience told you you have done much evil?" The king hung his head. "Ah," he sighed, "it is a terrible thing to be a king." Coillard then prayed with him. But still he was obdurate. He, however, became a total abstainer, and of his own accord forbade the manufacture, sale and drinking of beer in his kingdom—a lesson for Christian countries. He later tried to stop slavery also. Coillard was more hopeful of the king's son, Litia, who was hungry for learning and had considerable ability. Litia's faith gradually was undermined in the heathen superstitions. When one of the princes was ill and the mother ordered him to sacrifice at the ancestors' tombs for his recovery, Litia replied: "I am no longer in darkness, I no longer pray to the dead." Coillard frequently would say: "I do not see why Litia does not become an open Christian, for God's grace is evidently working in his heart."

The king in 1891 sent Litia to Basutoland to the French school there at Moriah, but he soon came suddenly back and startled Coillard by saying: "My father, I am no longer the old Litia. I am converted and have found Christ." It seems that Litia had come under the influence of a Christian chief, Khama, in that southern land and came home wanting to be like him.

Litia's conversion proved a great comfort to Mrs. Coillard. Ever since she had come to the land of the Barotsis her health had been failing. When the girls' school was started in addition to the boys' school, the king placed so many daughters and their servants in it that her private life was much interfered with. She said: "What a task to teach these filthy savages cleanliness, self-respect and morality!" And though the boys became impressed with Christianity, none of the girls did. Some of them she had to turn away for their immorality. In the midst of such surroundings she labored, and her health finally gave entirely away. A vacation was suggested to her after her break-down, but she heroically said: "Life is too short to abandon God's work for any such reason." On the Sunday before her death although weak, she went out into the field and was attacked by a vulture which she was almost too weak to resist. Help came, but she was brought into the village in a fainting condition. Still she recovered enough to attend both services. That evening she was filled with unspeakable joy as Litia made his public profession of Christ. And while he was speaking Mokomba, another young man of the royal family broke out into sobs. She said: "A Barotsi weeping, and weeping about his sins. I thought they had no tears to shed. Why, it is a sight I would have travelled 300 miles to see. It was the most beautiful meeting I have ever attended among the Zambesis."

It was to be her last. On Thursday they played and sang together "The Golden Gate:" as her husband afterwards said, " She had already sighted it." Then came the fever, making terrible progress. Her eyes filled with tears as she thought of leaving him alone among the savages. But before she died, on the eve of her death, she said to him: "Death is not as difficult as we thought and I feared. It is not painful, and then it is such a short passage when underneath are everlasting arms." She died October 28, 1891, gazing into the sky, as if she had a vision, and saying, "How very beautiful," and then saying, as they laid her on the bed, "I have at last arrived."

Great was the mourning in the mission and the villages as they laid her to rest. Her husband bears this testimony of her: "Much is said of the courage, activity and work of the missionary, but men ignore the fact that as a rule the missionary is a missionary only in proportion as his wife is one and assisting him." She was to him not only a wife, but a nurse, teacher, and really a martyr in her spirit. Writing to a friend about her death, he beautifully says "sursum corda": (Death is not a parting, but a reunion).

After her death came dark days. Litia soon went back to heathenish polygamy. The king, while he wanted the missionary to stay with him, yet hardened himself against religious influences. Coillard once said he knew the reality of martyrdom without its joys. Lewanika, the king, was a despot and insisted on forcing on the missionaries all sorts of exorbitant bargains. "What have I to do," he once said, "with a gospel that gives me neither guns, nor powder, nor coffee, nor tea, nor sugar, nor artisans to work for me?" Coillard says he was a weathercock; now favorable, now an enemy. He even proclaimed a blockade of the mission and threatened to strangle any one who served the missionary. The moral condition of the people oppressed Coillard. Once he wrote: "Heathen Africa can find no parallel to their state. The whole land is a Sodom and the benighted people whose conscience is dead, glory in their shame." The king finally inveigled the first convert, Nguana-Ngombe to his court and back to heathenism.

But in spite of all these difficulties the work grew. Some of the royal family became converted. On March 11, 1894, the church was dedicated and Litia began showing more interest. He came to the missionary, saying: "I want to be a child of God and I pray him to give me strength to be true to Him. Pray for me." Litia surprised them on Sunday, October 7, 1894, by rising in the large audience and saying: "Henceforth I have broken the bonds of Satan to become a child of God. I have sent away my second wife so as to obey God. Make haste and be converted to him." This act led to 120 conversions, among them several chiefs. Litia afterwards remained faithful to the church. In 1895 there was quite a revival, resulting in a number of converts.

In 1902 Coillard reported that "the chapel is often

quite full. Slaves carry in chairs for the chief, Litia, and his wife, and for the princess Akenangisod and her husband. Before the service the congregation is squatting outside of the chapel. When Litia passes, all kneel and clap their hands. He never replies to their salutations; for this would not be royal. He enters majestically following the missionary. Behind him comes a long procession of men who seat themselves on their mats, the young lads come in chattering and squat on the ground before the pulpit. Then, always late, comes the two princesses with their long train of women. The men are very attentive. To look at their faces you would say that they understood everything. They sing well, Litia especially. He also prays sometimes. He is very well mannered, has brilliant eyes and a pleasing smile. He is always well-dressed with a stiff collar, starched cuffs, dazzling shirt-front, black coat and polished shoes."

Perhaps one of the most touching stories of this mission is that told by a poor black woman at a prayer meeting, whose subject was "Lot's wife." She said she had just come up from the bottom of the valley. On her way she found people working in the fields on Sunday. She accosted them, and invited them to come and hear the word of God. They replied with contempt: "It is no longer the missionary who comes and reminds us that it is the Lord's day. Now it is these fag-ends of women folks. Begone! Be off to play the believer, if you imagine the missionaries are going to give you cloths and beads." "O, my masters," replied the poor thing, "I am nothing but a poor slave to be sure, I am nothing, but I feel the need of learning the things of God. Oh, no, it is not cloth or beads that I am looking for. What could I do with them? I have never worn anything but this bodice of skin. But I am a great sinner and what I seek is the pardon of my sins."

But the missionary's health began to break down. The Paris Society wanted him to come home on furlough, but he did not wish to do so, as he feared he might never return to the mission, as he was 60 years old. His reply to their request was: "Send us first ten workers and I will come and help you find ten others." But he was finally compelled by his health to take a vacation in 1896. When he left there were five stations in the Zambezi mission with a number of converts and a school of evangelists with 10 pupils. Before he left he was frequently visited by the king and others in his sickness. When Coillard said to the king that he mourned that he did not come out publicly as a Christain, the king replied: "That I am not a Christian is not your fault for you have given me no rest daily." Coillard arrived at Paris on June 18, 1896.

In 1899 he was again in Europe and when he left for the Zambesi (December 10, 1899), the Oratoire Church at Paris was crowded. The Rev. Theodore Monod said there that he would use of him the words engraven on the tomb of Charles Kingsley, "We have loved, we love, we will love." He had succeeded in raising nearly $30,000 in Europe for his mission and had gained a re-enforcement of fifteen missionaries. He is still hard at work in his field of the Zambesis.

At the recent coronation of King Edward VII of England, one of the foreign kings, whose visit awakened great interest, was King Lewanika, of Barotsiland. Though not a professing Christian, he is deeply concerned for the moral condition of his family, and is so favorable to them that he wrote to the Paris Mission Society from Edinburgh that he desired that country to be covered with a network of mission stations. He has succeeded in stamping out intemperance, the slave trade, and infanticide, and greatly raised the standard of civilization. Lewanika recently, on his return from the coronation of King Edward VII, at London, though still not a Christian, yet bore most remarkable testimony to it. In his address he said: "I have two words to say. Here is the first: 'Praise God, bless him.' For the second word I say, 'The Gospel—it is all.'" We trust he is not far from the kingdom of God.

Of his mission Rev. Dr. J. Johnson, of England, a competent authority says: "It is the most beautiful mission I have seen in Africa." Mr. Coillard tells a story that on one occasion when a pastor in Basutoland, a black minister, invited him to Kimberley, he went and greatly enjoyed the festival at the church. When he was about leaving the minister put into his hand a number of small diamonds. "These represent a day's work of my men. Choose which you like." Coillard says: "I took a long time to look over them. There were yellow, black and white. At last I chose a black one." "But that is the least valuable," said the minister. "Perhaps so," said Coillard, but I like black diamonds; they are the jewels I am seeking myself for the Saviour's crown." He will wear many black diamonds in his crown of rejoicing in heaven as the witness of his work.

Chapter V.

PAUL BERTHOUD AND ERNEST CREUX.

Sometimes missionaries go in pairs and become twins in the work—true yoke-fellows in Christ. The southwestern part of Switzerland is French and the Free Churches of the three French cantons, of Neuchatel, Vaud and Geneva, have united to form a Missionary Society, which they called the Romande Society. The beginnings of their organization came about in this way. In May, 1869, the Synod of the Free Church of the canton of Vaud, at its session at Lausanne, was taken by surprise at receiving a challenge from two of the students of their Theological Seminary at Lausanne, Paul Berthoud and Ernst Creux, in which they offered themselves as foreign missionaries. (Neither of the French-Swiss churches had as yet its own mission, although they had raised some money which they paid into the treasury of the Mission Society at Paris). The letter was a fine specimen of youthful earnestness for the salvation of the heathen. "To whom shall we go," said the letter, "rather than to the church to which we belong? We will go wherever you wish us—to the tropics in the south, or to the regions of ice in the north. Speak, command, send, and we will obey."

The synod was deeply moved by this earnest appeal, but felt itself too small a body to undertake so great a work as to start a missionary society of its own and send these young men. The deliberateness of older heads halted the effort to advance. But the next synod at St. Croix (held the same year), appointed a committee of five to aid the young men in carrying out their desire and immediately money began to flow in for the work.

While the Vaud Church was deliberating and the young men were waiting, the Paris Missionary Society sent word to them: "Why do you hold back the young men so long? Send them to us. We can use them." So finally in 1872, three years after their first appeal, the two young men, Berthoud and Creux, went to South Africa to engage in service for the Paris Society. But they were not to remain in its service long, for Rev. Mr. Mabille, one of the Paris Society's missionaries, had gone on an exploring tour northward to a new district called the Ma-Gwamba. He brought this district to the notice of the Paris Society, but it found itself too weak to undertake this new work, and it appealed to the Free Church of Vaud to take it as its mission. So finally on April 28, 1874, the Synod of that church decided to form a missionary society of its own and to appoint Berthoud and Creux as its missionaries and send them to the Ma-Gwamba. The missionaries at once set out for this country located in the northeastern part of the Transvaal, and on July 9, 1875, they arrived at Spelonken and began living among the savages. They at once found that the first necessity was the learning of a new language, the Ma-gwamba, which they soon reduced to writing. They called the mission Valdezia, naming it after their canton of Vaud.

They found the natives willing to learn. In studying the language they found that the blacks had traditions of the flood which had come down to them. Beginning with this trace of Bible story they tried to lead the poor savages up to the Bible and to Jesus. A great hindrance, however, was the immoral character of the blacks. They were given to stealing, lying and immorality. They were also superstitious and much under control of their medicine men, who, of course, bitterly opposed the missionaries. But the missionaries bravely continued to visit the villages and to hold service, and in course of time one-fortieth of the people attended worship and some became catechumens. Creux took charge of the school and Berthoud of the catechumens and the sick, as he had some knowledge of medicine.

Then another difficulty appeared. The Transvaal government in June, 1876, forbade them to preach to the natives without its express permission. They declared this impossible, for it was for that purpose that they had come to Africa. They would rather obey the voice of God than of man. Finally they were arrested for their refusal to obey the government and were sent to prison, August 1, at Marastabad. Their arrest was so sudden that they were compelled to leave their wives and children behind them in the wilderness at the mission station. Unfortunately just at that time war broke out near Spelonken and their families were left without any defense. From the mission station their wives were so close to hostilities that they could see the burning of villages and the battles, and also the processions of fugitives, near enough to hear the fusillade of the battle and the cries of the wounded. Great was their anxiety, but their covenant-God took care of them. The missionaries themselves were treated kindly in their prison, more as guests than as prisoners, and were allowed to preach to the blacks where they were imprisoned. Finally on September 6, 1876, after a little over a month's imprisonment, they were set free and allowed to return to Spelonken.

As soon as they had returned evidences of the presence of God's Spirit began to show themselves. Three weeks later, on October 1, they had their first baptism which took place a little over a year after their arrival at the mission. Their first convert was a poor black woman named Sehlumula. She had been maltreated by her husband and had been driven away from home by him in scorn. She had seen all her children die. She had been at the mercy of a cruel and violent brother, who intended to sell her as a slave so as to make some money off of her. In all her troubles she at last found comfort in Jesus. At her baptism she told the story of her conversion which produced a great effect on her hearers. She received the name of Lydia, because like Lydia in Paul's time, she was their first convert in the new continent. On July 8, 1877, seven more were received into the church and by the end of 1878 there were 40 baptized Christians. In 1878 a new station named Elim was founded, and in 1879 Creux took charge of it.

But the mission still suffered afflictions. Sickness and even death came into their midst. Mrs. Berthoud was called away by death and also some of the missionaries' children. But while Providence was decreasing their number by death, it was increasing it by sending out new missionaries. Who should be sent out from Switzerland but the brother of Bethoud, Henry. Finally in 1883 the Free Churches of the other French cantons, (Neuchatel and Geneva), united with this society of the Canton Vaud in forming a united society, which they called the Romande Society. This gave it a much larger constituency at home and the work in Africa was correspondingly enlarged. New missionaries were sent and the work rapidly grew in prosperity and influence.

But the most successful field of this Missionary Society was at Delagoa Bay on the east coast of Africa. As early as 1880 one of the new converts named Joseph happened to go to Delagoa Bay in search of his sisters whom he had not seen for 25 years, until they succeeded in escaping from slavery together with their mother. He returned to the Ma-

Gwamba, but in 1881 he was again sent to Delagoa Bay by Creux to sound the chief there and find out whether he could be favorable to the starting of a new mission. Joseph came back with bright news, saying that the field was full of promise. The missionaries decided to send him there as an evangelist. On April 23 he was ordained at Spelonken when the converted heathen raised money to start this new mission station. They called the new mission Antioch, because like Antioch in Scripture, it was the first attempt of the converted to establish a mission elsewhere. About the same time that Antioch was founded, a brother-in-law of Joseph, named Eliaschib, founded another station south of Antioch at Rikatla.

This whole district has been called a white man's grave on account of the awful mortality there to the whites. Nevertheless in 1887 Paul Berthoud visited the field. As he neared the coast he was surprised to hear singing in the language of the Ma-Gwamba. It was the people of Rikatla, 130 in number, who, under Joseph's leadership, had come out to meet him. He was greatly moved by this kind reception and much encouraged in view of the dangers to him there. He finally, in the face of the African fever so prevalent, settled right there. But a kind Providence watched over him and the fever did not touch him. Soon a most remarkable religious movement began in the Delagoa Bay region. At Tempe, the farthest point from the mission, there was a man named Jim Boy. He had been baptized, but had fallen from grace, being a polygamist and slave-trader. Still the influence of Christianity remained with him, for he would preach, and the natives under him were so much moved that great weeping occurred at his services. He returned to the church afterwards.

At Rikatla also very remarkable scenes took place. Eliaschib's house was the meeting-place for worship. When a man was met on the way to it and was asked, "Where are you going," his reply would be, "To the spring." And when asked "Why?" he would answer, "Because I am thirsty." Having arrived at Eliaschib's house he would seat himself among the people and say, "I am hungry." Then the Bible would be brought out and explained, and his hunger appeased. How simple-hearted the piety of these blacks. What an example to many in our Christian lands, who, in spite of all their Christian privileges, hunger and thirst so little for

The Reformed Church. 143

the privileges of worship. These converts called themselves "The Children of the Lord," "Children of the Father," and "God's Beloved Ones." A great revival followed in which, it is true, there were some extravagences, for some became inspirationists and declared that they saw visions. All through the movement it required the most careful guidance, which Berthoud was able to give it. But the result of it was that in 1888 300 united with the church. In 1889 Berthoud founded another mission at Lorenzo Marque, the seaport of Delagoa Bay.

But dangers threatened the whole mission. War broke out in 1894 between the Portuguese and the blacks. Many of their out-stations were destroyed. Some of the Christians were killed, among them an evangelist, Galasa, who was speared while kneeling in prayer. But after the war it continued to prosper. In 1898 it had 8 stations, 12 married missionaries with 8 other missionaries. Its membership had risen to 1,800, of whom 1,000 were at Lorenzo Marque. The Missionary Society at home raised that year $30,000, of which $5,000 were given for the famine then raging in South Africa. Of this the mission itself raised $1,275. For the natives were very liberal, considering their poverty. Thus on one occasion, after Creux had preached, a young man stepped up and gave him $80, saying it was part of the money he had once received for a stolen diamond. He said: "I can no longer endure the guilt of it. Here is the money, and the remaining $20 I will bring as soon as I am able." So great a reputation did these black Christians gain for honesty that the European merchants would ask the missionaries for men to whom they could entrust money to buy cattle in the interior. There are now over 2,000 members in the mission, of whom the greater part are in the region of Delagoa Bay.

"Great," says Rev. Mr. Grandjean, one of the missionaries who has been recalled from Africa to become the home secretary of the Society in Switzerland, "great have been the changes. Among the sheaves were some very remarkable ones. At the Littoral we see a number of women whom we love to call mothers in Israel, a Lois, who, for example, has been the living centre of those at Rikatla, and at Lorenzo Marque, a Sarah, whose house had formerly been a house of infamy, but now the first place of worship. We have seen a great number of men change their lives from laziness to activity and regularity. We have seen heathen chiefs abandoning their pagan lives of voluptuousness and becoming Christians at the risk of losing their prestige and position, as Jim at Tempe, Mohlaba at Schlouvane, and Ndjakandjaka at Spelonken. We have seen a large number of young men drawn from a pagan life to become evangelists after seven years of study in two strange languages, the Sessouto and the English. We have seen transformations in the individual, in society, in the relations between the tribes, and in the attitude of the government."

Chapter VI.
ESCANDE AND MINAULT.
THE REFORMED MARTYRS OF THE 19TH CENTURY.

Madagascar has been the scene of wonderful success, of terrible persecutions and magnificent martyrdoms—"a nation born in a day," as her people so wonderfully welcomed Christianity. Then came the awful persecutions, 1835-61, especially on March 28, 1849, when 14 native Christians bound with ropes were thrown over the "Stone of Hurling," a precipice 100 feet high, at the capital, Antananarivo. But the blood of the martyrs is the seed of the church, and when the missionaries returned in 1861 they found the number of Christians had greatly increased in their absence, as in the capital they had risen from 200 in 1835 to 700 in 1861. The London Society had a few years ago 60,000 communicants and 300,000 adherents in Madagascar, and there are other societies also laboring there, as the Friends and Norwegians.

But for the last few years, evil times have fallen on that island. France for nearly a century has had her eye on this rich island and sought every opportunity to gain influence there. In 1883 she attacked her but gained nothing except a resident general at the capital with a few French troops as a guard of honor. Finally in 1895 France sent an army of 15,000 to subjugate the island. They landed and marched to the capital 300 miles inland. They met with practically no opposition, losing far more by sickness than by war. Fears were early entertained that if France gained control the fine work of the London Missionary Society would be interfered with and perhaps stopped. And so it came to pass. Although the French government did not forbid Protestant missions in its colonies as it had done in the early part of the nineteenth century (for Frances' influence has always been with Catholicism), yet the Catholics at once saw their opportunity in Madagascar. And with the French army came the Catholic priests, especially the Jesuits. However, fortunately for the Protestants, the first French Governor-General there happened to be a Protestant, Mr. Laroche. For this the Romanists cursed the home government because it interfered with their unlimited control. Still in certain districts there was much oppression—the Catholic worship introduced and the Protestant forced out. The Protestant evangelists were driven out and missionaries evicted from their parsonages. The Catholics especially fostered the idea that the missionaries of the London Missionary Society, being foreigners and Englishmen, were disloyal to the new French government. Gallieni, the French general said: "All Protestants are Englishmen and ought to be shot."

But at that juncture of affairs the London Society proposed to turn over its work to the Paris Society, as it was French, so that the splendid Protestant movement might not be checked. It was too large a field for the latter society. Nevertheless they rose to the opportunity at once as far as they were able. Some missions were transferred, enough to show the government that the London Society had no selfish aims or wished to be disloyal to France. The Paris Society, as soon as the island came under the power of France, sent two French pastors thither, Lauga and Kruger, who began holding French Protestant services there. Their presence was a great gain; for the Jesuits had gone about saying: "All Protestants are Englishmen and are to be shot and all Catholics are Frenchmen and are to be saved or promoted." Their presence proved to the natives that there were Protestants among the French.

However under General Gallieni the native Protestants suffered considerable oppression. From the beginning Protestant churches there were used by the soldiers as barracks, but none of the Catholic churches. Then the government proceeded farther —to take other mission buildings for state use. In Betsileo province the people were terrorized shamelessly by the agents of the Jesuits. The missionaries of the London Missionary Society were banished on the plea that they were Hovas (natives of Madagascar). The twelve leading men of one church were banished because suspicion was raised against them that they were friendly to the English.

The Paris Missionary Society at once proceeded to send missionaries there, who took charge of the Protestant primary schools of the London Society, for which there were 500 with more than 30,000 scholars. Their missionaries had not been long there when two of them won the crown of martyrdom, Mr. Escande and Mr. Minault, who were cruelly massacred on the road from the capital to Fianarantsoa, where the latter was about to occupy the mission station in the disturbed district of Betsileo.

Rev. Benjamin Escande was one of the best mis-

REV. BENJAMIN ESCANDE.

sionaries of the Paris Society. He had been missionary for a number of years in the French colony of the Senegal in West Africa. He was born at Mazainet, France, December 6, 1864. At a very early age he manifested a love for spiritual things. "Mamma," he said, when eight years old, "I would like to be a deacon." God made him more than that—a missionary. But this showed his early desire for religious work. It was however the visit of the famous missionary Coillard to France in 1881 that led him definitely to determine to become a missionary. His parents did not for a moment oppose his choice but said: "Our Benjamin has been consecrated to Jesus since his birth. Let Him do with him as seemeth best." After preparatory studies in his home in France he was ordained at Paris November 27, 1888, at the Church of the Oratoire in Paris. He settled at St. Louis, in Sengal, Africa, where he labored faithfully and successfully about eight years.

In 1896, during a furlough in Europe, the Paris Missionary Society appealed for volunteers for Madagascar who would defend religious liberty there and protect the Protestant church then menaced by the Jesuits. They desired some one to go, as Messrs. Kruger and Lauga were about to return home. Not finding any person for such an urgent and delicate mission, the Committee of the Paris Missionary Society appealed to Escande to go. Although at home in order to recruit his health, he at once responded to their request by the telegram, "I am at the disposition of the Committee. As God directs you." He sailed from Marseilles August 26, 1896, and arrived at Antananarivo September 26, 1896. He was kept very busy trying to regain the churches of which the Protestants had been dispossessed and to make the government respect the liberty of conscience of the Protestants. In this he showed great tact, courage and perseverance. In every way he tried to bring to naught the designs of the Jesuits. He labored at Antananarivo as French pastor and preacher, and besides had also a large correspondence with the mission churches at the home Society in France. Paul Minault, who was a new missionary, a young man, said of him one day: "He is a hero. I am filled beyond bounds with admiration for him." The new missionaries he awaited with great joy. They arrived at Antananarivo April 26, 1897—five of them: Minault, Delord, Moudain, Meyer and Ducommun.

The Reformed Church. 153

A few days after this the missionaries held their conference, at which Minault was appointed to Finanarantsoa, the capital of Betsileo province where the Protestant work was dying through the intrigues of the Jesuits. Escande accompanied him in his journey because the young man's health had been weakened by violent attacks of fever. They left Antananarivo May 17, 1897. On May 21 after dinner they arrived in the gorges of Anharatra, nearly thirty miles from the capital. After a halt of two hours for dinner they continued their journey. But when they had gone about a mile, their convoy was suddenly assailed by thirty armed bandits from an ambuscade. Their men at once threw down their loads and escaped in every direction. The two missionaries, accompanied by the faithful boy of Mr. Escande, Rainimanga, tried in vain to escape the assassins. Escande was ahead riding. Minault, weakened by the fever and the too heavy clothing, was unable to escape by running. He fell without a word when the fatal shot struck him. Escande, who had dismounted from his horse to aid his companion when he saw him fall, tried to remount to escape but was not able. He took several steps when in turning he fell, struck by a ball.

The boy, happily, recovered the horse of Mr. Escande and brought the sad news to Ramainandro where there was a French military post. The bodies were found with many spear wounds upon them, where they had been speared after they had been shot. They were buried there and their colleagues placed the inscription on their tomb, "To our Friends B. Escande and P. Minault, assassinated May 21, 1897. 'I have fought the good fight.'" The French government later placed a monument to them.

Their loss turned out to be a blessing in disguise. The French government learned to respect the Protestants. And it was a bugle-blast to the French Reformed at home. Their old Huguenot blood rose within them. The Church rose from its stupor and rallied with far greater energy to the support of this mission. At once many volunteers in France offered to take their places. The mission in Madagascar will ever be dear to French Protestants because baptized with blood. The Paris Society now has a very successful mission in Madagascar to which the French government has been making amends and French newspapers have paid a tribute that their schools there were better than those of the Romanists. The result has been that the success of the Catholics has been checked. In one district where there had been six Catholic churches and one of the London Mission, now the Catholic churches have been closed and the London Society has six churches. Thus the French Reformed saved the Protestant church of Madagascar and enriched it with the blood of the martyrs.

BOOK III.

THE REFORMED IN ASIA.
A.— India.

CHAPTER I.
ALPHONSE F. LACROIX.

AN unknown and forgotten Reformed missionary is Lacroix,—unknown, because he lived so far away and so long ago; forgotten, because his name is dimmed by the lustre of great missionaries so much better known to us. And yet what Judson was to America, what Carey was to England, Lacroix was to the French-speaking Reformed churches of Switzerland—the John the Baptist to awaken them to their responsibility to save the heathen. He was a great missionary, and if the Reformed Church forgets to honor him, she is the loser by it. He was a native of French Switzerland, born near the scene of the labors of Farel, that Elijah of the Alps in Reformation days. What Farel did three hundred years before in stirring up that region to a new life in the gospel, that Lacroix did there in the last century, stirring it to new life for foreign missions. He is interesting to English readers, and especially to those interested in woman's work, because he is the father of Mrs. Mullens, who is reputed to have been the founder of mission work among the Zenanas of India, where so many thousands of women are imprisoned without hope or love. The story is this,* —that Mrs. Mullens sat one day in her parlor embroidering a pair of slippers for her husband. A Brahmin gentleman greatly admired them. Mrs. Mullens asked him if he would not like to have his wife taught to make them. He answered, "Yes." So she went to his wife and began to teach her the embroidering of slippers, but with it she intertwined the teaching of God's Word and of Jesus' love. As some one says: "A needle opened the way to reach the millions of India." Other Brahmin women wanted to learn to embroider slippers, so her opportunities increased. Other Zenanas were opened until now there are a number of Zenana societies with scores of missionaries who are visiting and brightening up those Eastern prisons with the tidings of Christ's love.

Alphonse Francis Lacroix was born May 10, 1799, at Lignieres, in the canton of Neuchatel,

---

*This origin of Zenana work has been denied, and the denial of it is probably so far true that she was not the originator of work for women in India as others urged it before her. Still the story is very beautiful.

Switzerland. As his father died soon after his birth, his uncle took charge of him. His uncle had charge of a boarding school in the suburbs of Neuchatel, and was one of the few godly men in that age of unbelief who was not afraid to confess Christ. His school, therefore, had an atmosphere of piety about it that did not fail to tell on his nephew. Indeed, the Christian influence of this uncle was the original cause in preparing him ultimately to become a missionary. There by the stone of Serrieres where Farel stood when he first preached the doctrines of the reformation in that canton, he learned the earnest truths of that gospel, so as to preach them to the heathen. His uncle, anxious to have him learn German, sent him to Zurich, where he lived in the family of one of the pastors. He learned German, but the spiritual influence of that home was not what his uncle's school was. For alas! the Church of Zwingli had become cold through rationalistic influences in the early part of this century. He returned to Neuchatel when twelve years of age.

Here the boy was father of the man, and early revealed his future characteristics. He possessed immense energy and incessant activity, and his tall, stout, well-knit form seemed capable of doing endless work and bearing great fatigue. Many deeds of daring are told of him. On one occasion he was almost drowned. He lost his senses in the water, and afterwards described how in a moment of time the whole of his past life passed before him. He was, however, saved for great purposes, like Wesley. War had a great fascination for him. He longed to become a soldier. The bravery of Arnold Winkelried at Sempach, where he fell pierced by the Austrian spears a martyr-hero for Switzerland, enthused him. In this there was danger that he would be drawn off from what was to become his life work afterwards as a missionary. Yet it is not wonderful that he was inclined that way. For his boyhood took place during the stirring scenes of the wars of Napoleon. Even down to his old age he never forgot an old general of eighty years of age reviewing a body of troops. His uncle, however, was averse to soldier life, and wanted him to enter the ministry. For that purpose he placed him at one of the colleges in Neuchatel.

And now occurs a crisis in his history. The military fever ran so high that when fourteen years of age he resolved to join a Swiss regiment in the

French army. He, however, like a dutiful boy, went to his uncle to get his permission before he went. The uncle refused for a while, but finally reluctantly gave his consent. Lacroix started with his knapsack to go to Berne, thirty miles away, to enlist. Meanwhile his uncle, who believed that the effectual, fervent prayer of the righteous availeth much, went to praying. As the young recruit neared Berne, and was almost within sight of the city, a sudden change came over him. It seemed to him as if a hand were laid on his shoulder, and a voice rang in his heart, as came to Elijah: "What dost thou here? Return!" He paused, obeyed and turned back. When he came home, he flung himself into the arms of his uncle, saying: "Ah, dear uncle, you have been praying for me. I know you have been calling me back. Here I am." He was not to be a soldier of Napoleon, but a soldier of a greater than Napoleon, who conquers not by the sword, but by the sword of the Spirit. This incident made a marked change in his character. His religious life deepened. He became more spiritually minded. He was especially helped just at that time by Jung Stilling's book, "Scenes in the Kingdom of Spirits," and ever after that great German writer remained a favorite of his.

Two years later another incident occurred in his life that was another link in forging the chain to lead him into the mission field. He was called away from Switzerland to be tutor in a private family at Amsterdam, where he lived for three years. There was great interest in Holland at that time in missions. Here it was that he was brought into contact directly with foreign missions; for missionary prayer meetings were held there under the influence of the Netherlands Missionary Society. It was while attending a prayer meeting, where the overthrow of idolatry in the Sandwich Islands was described, that he first felt the desire to become a missionary. For six months he prayed over this, before he breathed it to others. Then it became so great a burden to him that he wrote to his uncle for advice. The uncle was only too glad to approve of his entrance into such religious work.

The Netherlands Society had sent out a call for three missionaries. He applied, was accepted and then enrolled as a student for a year and a half at their Mission House at Berkel, in Holland. When he was about to enter the mission field it happened that a pious physician, Dr. Vos, had come from India to Holland and asked that a missionary be

The Reformed Church.   165

sent to the few towns in India still remaining under the control of the Dutch. So he was ordered to go to Chinsurah in India. On August 11, 1820, he was ordained a minister of the Dutch Reformed Church at the Hague, and on August 25 a farewell service was held in the French Reformed church at Rotterdam, where Rev. Van Oordt solemnly presented the missionary with a Bible and urged him to preach its solemn truths. He sailed from England for India October 1, 1820, and landed at Chinsurah March 2, 1821.

The town of Chinsurah was an old Dutch town with about one hundred Dutch houses, the rest being native and Oriental. There was little religious influence there. Three missionaries of the London Missionary Society were already laboring there; but of the foreigners some were infidels and many of them immoral. The Dutch governor gave him quarters at the Government House. He began to study the language very assiduously, and joined himself very closely to Rev. Mr. Townley, one of the London Society's missionaries, going with him on his missionary tours. Almost the first sight he saw was a suttee, or the burning of a widow. Mr. Townley expostulated with the family although there was a large crowd present, but it had no effect. The widow was burned before their eyes. The impression of this horror of the Hindoo system Lacroix never forgot during all his life. On another occasion he saw a man drowning, and he called to a boat to pick him up, but they refused for fear they would break their caste by touching him, and so he drowned. No wonder he despised and exposed a religion that sanctioned that.

He soon began to teach in one of the Dutch public schools at Chinsurah, taking charge of the school. Although his instructions were in secular studies, yet he did not forget to train his pupils in that wisdom that cometh from above. Indeed a beautiful illustration is told that thirty years after when he was preaching in a Presbyterian church at Agra, at the close of the service a gentleman, employed in one of the government offices, came up to him, his eyes streaming with tears, to present his thanks for all the kind care received from him in that school so many years before, and to express his intense delight at so unexpectedly seeing his face and hearing his voice once more. He was an elder in that church, and attributed all the religious impressions that led him to Christ to the instruction of Lacroix in his school. Lacroix thanked God and took courage, remembering the promise, "Cast thy bread upon the waters, and it shall return after many days."

Another prominent line of work at Chinsurah was preaching to the natives. This the missionaries of the London Society had been doing, and in two years he was able to join them in this and preach too. They preached in the school houses, especially about the hour of sunset. They would preach the simple gospel, but would often be interrupted by opponents.

On one of these occasions Lacroix witnessed an amusing incident. Mr. Mundy had been preaching to a large crowd under the branches of a spreading tree, when an old Brahmin, who did not like to see the people so attentive to the Christian preacher, asked in a faultfinding tone: "What was the use of talking to all these people? They were poor, and why did not the preacher do something more sensible by relieving their bodily wants, than by preaching?" "Very true," said Mr. Mundy, "it is right to assist the destitute, and as you Brahmin have no hat—here, take mine." And, suiting the action to the word, without giving him time to object, Mr.

Mundy put his old hat on the Brahmin's head and pressed it down. The latter was horrified at this, for by it he broke caste by touching what belonged to a Christian. Discomfited he hastened off, amid the laughter of the people, who were greatly delighted at the joke. On another occasion, after Lacroix had preached, Mr. Mundy was about to distribute tracts, when, as the people pressed him so closely, he climbed into a tree that he might give them singly and more conveniently. When to the delight of the people, the bottom of the basket came out, the tracts fell with it, and after a violent scramble among the people, they were carried off in triumph.

Another sphere of labor for Lacroix was among the foreigners at Chinsurah, who were dependent on missionaries for preaching. The missionaries preached in English and Lacroix in Dutch every Sunday. He found, however, considerable difficulty in doing this at first, because the Holland language was not his mother-tongue. On one occasion he began preaching and announced that he would divide his sermon into four heads. But, alas, as he proceeded he forgot what was the last head, and had to finish the sermon abruptly. He was the more discouraged by this, because Dr. Vos, one of the directors of his Missionary Society, happened to be present. But to his astonishment, Dr. Vos said to him the next evening that it was a good sermon and that the illustrations were particularly full and striking.

But the time came when his sphere was to be changed. The few Dutch colonies in India came under the control of the English government in 1825. The Netherlands Missionary Society felt that it should not do missionary work in English territory, when it had such wide fields in Java and the East Indies, which were under its own government. Besides, that excellent and venerable society began, alas, to feel the effects of rationalism that denied Christ's divinity and man's depravity, and which was coming into Holland. This was cutting the nerve of the missionary zeal, and the Society was beginning, therefore, to lose its first love. For if the Church at home does not believe in total depravity, then it does not believe the heathen are depraved enough to have missionaries sent to them. And if it does not believe in the divinity of Christ, He is not good enough to be offered to them. The Netherlands Society therefore discontinued its missions in

India, and gave Lacroix the choice of going to Java or of entering some other society, if he wished to stay in India. He chose the latter alternative, retired from the Society and joined the London Missionary Society in 1827, with whose missionaries he had all along been so intimately associated in India. He was, therefore, for six years a missionary of the Dutch Reformed Society. But although no longer a missionary of the Reformed Church, yet his influence in the Reformed Church of the continent, especially in his native land, was so great that we will continue his life.

In 1829 he removed from Chinsurah to Calcutta. He there engaged extensively in preaching and in itinerating. For his great knowledge of the Bengali language made him one of the most eloquent and effective preachers in India. He could always gain a large audience by the charm of his voice, by his beautiful use of their language and the beautiful imagery in which he clothed his ideas. He also superintended several congregations south of Calcutta at Rammakalchoke and Gungree, eight and twelve miles from Calcutta. He labored in them twelve years, going to them in heat and cold, in storm and pleasant weather.

Many were his discouragements. In May, 1833, one of the most awful hurricanes that was ever known burst over Bengal. A series of terrible waves, ten feet high, burst into the land, sweeping everything for more than fifty miles inland. Twenty thousand persons were drowned. The rich harvest was lost, and so famine and pestilence followed the hurricane. For several weeks long rows of starving people were fed daily at his garden. Wherever he went out among the villages, he carried bags of pica (an Indian cent) to distribute among the crowds. And yet in the midst of all the discouragements the mission had a steady growth. During the twelve years from 1829-1841 one hundred and twenty members were added, and the Christian community rose from fifty to four hundred. In January, 1837, he moved to Blowanpore, the southern suburb of Calcutta, so as to found there a missionary station with a school for the sons of his converts. He was too wise a man not to see that the subtle Indian mind must be met by education as well as evangelization. This school proved so successful that the London Society made it their principal mission in Calcutta. Here the boys were trained to become preachers of the gospel. His wife also started a school for the poor Hindu girls, which was also a wonderful success in numbers, reaching to five hundred. But as the girls were not allowed to stay longer than when ten years of age, it was given up, because it could bring few returns.

But Mr. Lacroix, although a diligent teacher, was most of all a preacher of the gospel. His tall, commanding presence and his powerful voice always made a deep impression on the simple people to whom he preached. To these were added a clear pronunciation of the Bengali language. His style of sermon was Scriptural, powerful, personal. A servant once told his mistress that whenever Mr. Lacroix preached, every Bengali's heart trembled. For nearly thirty years he was considered the most elegant preacher in Bengali that the country contained. Indeed, so great was his eloquence that efforts were made to set him free from any particular mission, so that he might devote his time entirely to preaching and evangelizing among the villages. This was done during the years 1836-1837, and he greatly enjoyed it.

Their method of holding services would seem odd and strange to us. Thus he would go into one of the bazaar chapels and begin reading from a desk a selection from the Bible. This he explains. During his explanation perhaps ten or fifteen persons come in. He then begins to preach. He takes no text, but describes some story from the Bible. He expounds it, illustrates it by incidents, argues and enforces it. The hearers listen with attention. Sometimes one will object, and he must be answered at once, or the preacher will not carry his audience with him. If they are interested, they remain, and at a striking argument, or a pointed story or a good humored exposure of their gods, will laugh or cry out "capital." If not interested, they go out, but others come in to take their places, and so there is a perpetual coming and going during the service. The preacher must be careful to repeat his theme a number of times, so that the late ones may know what he is talking about. Lacroix usually preaches about three-quarters of an hour. After the sermon he offers a short prayer, and the people gather to receive tracts and gospels. Thus he scatters the seeds. A few remain as inquirers, or show their interest by coming again and again. These are followed up, and by and by perhaps are gathered into the Church.

On one occasion, at the Simlia chapel, he had been arguing with a man who was a Pantheist. For the Hindus believe in Pantheism, namely, that all things are God. The man was very stubborn and would receive nothing advanced against his views. Mr. Lacroix therefore said he would no more argue, and, before the whole congregation suddenly seizing the man's umbrella, began walking out of the chapel. The man called after him and said, "That is my umbrella." "Your umbrella, did you say? Have you not declared that Brahma is everything, that he is you and I and all the people? How then can there be such a thing as mine and yours? The umbrella is mine as much as it is yours on your own showing." The people laughed at this clever argument, and the man was silenced and left the place without a word. The discussion was conducted in good temper, for the purpose of showing the real errors of the Hindu creed. Often he touched his audience very sharply. On one occasion he was preaching a sermon on lying, on the story of Ananias and Sapphira; as he pressed home the illustrations of judgment given in God's Word, the people were spell-bound and a profound impression was produced on them. And when he finished with a brief closing prayer, a stranger, who had never entered the bazaar chapel before, rose up with a deep sigh, which said as plainly as words could express it: "Well, that is the finest thing I ever heard in my life."

Lacroix was generally very gladly heard by the natives, but only on one occasion was injury offered to him, which but for the protection of his Master might have been severe. He was preaching one evening in the chapel in Pontonia in Calcutta, when, without any reason furnished by himself, a Hindu fanatic came quietly behind him and with a big stick aimed a blow at his head, so that he would knock him down. Providentially at that moment Lacroix turned, and the blow fell on his shoulder. The people jumped up in a minute and seized the man, calling aloud for a police. But Lacroix stopped them, and then, placing the man in front of the crowd, without a particle of anger in his voice or manner, he thus addressed him: "You have endeavored to do me a severe injury, and I might justly complain against you and have you punished. But the religion I preach teaches me to forgive those who do me harm. For the sake of that religion, therefore, I forgive you and will let you go away." This simple incident produced a far deeper impression and called forth a louder demonstration than any sermon he had ever preached. Struck with the exceeding kindness of his act, the audience in the chapel, Hindus though they were, at once burst into a loud shout: "Victory! victory, through Jesus Christ!" "Greater is he that ruleth his spirit than he that taketh a city."

Lacroix seems to have been a fearless man, for he would often meet large cobras lying in the sun. He had no fear of them, when he had a stick in his hand and boots on his feet. On one occasion, when he stayed in the chapel over night, a snake was crawling along the floor and approaching the table. He put his arm out of the mosquito curtain and seized his boot to throw at the visitor. But just at that moment the light went out, and he was compelled to leave him alone. Not being at all nervous, he tucked the curtains in carefully and fearlessly fell asleep.

After having been in India for nearly twenty years, he was at length compelled to return to Europe. Though his strong, robust frame seemed to be able to bear any great labor and fatigue, yet the intense heat of India, which affects especially the nervous system, began to tell on his health. In these days the missionary societies have retreats in the Himalaya mountains, to which their worn out missionaries can go, but in those days they knew nothing of such things. The sick, worn out missionaries had to return home. Lacroix therefore sailed from India and arrived in England in April, 1842. But he found himself a stranger there, as he had never met any of the Board of his Missionary Society. For he had gone out under another Society, the Netherlands, and now for the first time he met the directors of his own Society, the London Missionary Society. They treated him very kindly, but his sympathies were on the continent where his friends and relatives lived. With all the home-sickness of the Swiss he longed to see his native Alps again, and he soon traveled up the Rhine to the land of his birth. He found that the Swiss Churches had been very little interested in missions, except at Basle, where almost the first missionary society on the continent had been formed in the latter part of the last century. Especially were the French or southern cantons of Switzerland ignorant on the subject of missions. Only at Geneva, where a few earnest Christians had formed a sort of auxiliary to the Basle missionary society, was there any interest taken. This had been somewhat deepened by the visit of Gobat, the missionary to Abyssinia.

It remained for Lacroix to stir up the interest and produce a wonderful missionary revival in French Switzerland. He came to Geneva just as the interest in missions seemed to be deepening. In June he visited the old home of his boyhood in Neuchatel. What tender memories gathered around his uncle's school and the old Reformed church there, which he had joined. He then returned to Basle, to assist in the ordination of five missionaries, and his address on that occasion made a deep impression. But the Committee of the Basle Society, that had its headquarters at Geneva, asked him to deliver a course of lectures on missions. They arranged to have them in a small church holding about two hundred persons. But the interest of the people in missions was greater than the faith of those who projected the course of lectures. For half an hour before the first lecture began, the church was packed and as many more were waiting outside of the church for admission. They therefore adjourned to a neighboring hall, where four hundred listened to his account of the strange faith of the Hindus. Lacroix described this with all his popular eloquence, which swayed his audience before him. His remarks made such an impression that at the second lecture the audience had doubled, and when he delivered the third lecture, a thousand persons were present, including the leading ministers of Geneva. And they hung breathless on his eloquence as he described the progress made by the leading Indian missionaries. Now the audience was moved to laughter, now to tears, by his apt words and bright illustrations. The attendance kept on increasing at each lecture, until at the fifth lecture not only was the hall filled, but the stairs and lobbies, and people stood where they could hear his voice even if they could not see him.

These were wonderful experiences for Geneva, that city which had been so injured by rationalism at the close of the last and the beginning of this century. And it was strange that such a rationalistic, worldly city could be stirred in this way, especially on missions, at which so many had doubted, yes, sneered. They were the talk of the city and of the whole neighborhood. Never before had Geneva been so stirred on the subject of missions. It was a sort of resurrection of Calvin's interest; for he, centuries before, had sent out two Reformed ministers from Geneva as the first Foreign Missionaries to Brazil. The missionary committee who had charge of these lectures felt that they had gained so much influence that they made bold to ask for one of the largest churches in the city for the closing lecture. This was rather a presumptuous undertaking, for the State Church had been honeycombed with rationalism, and many of its ministers had looked down on Foreign Missions as the dream of the enthusiast.

But, strange to say, the Venerable Company of Pastors, which controlled all the state churches, granted the request and placed the Madeline church at the disposal of the committee. This was a church which had rung with the eloquence of Farel, the Elijah of the Alps, in the days of the Reformation. When Sunday, October 28, 1842, came, that church was filled in every part, so that seats had to be carried into the aisles, and the stairways and door were thronged with people. It is believed that there were not less than 3,000 persons present. Never since the days of Farel had that church been so thronged.

On the large platform around the pulpit sat the ministers of both the Free and the State Church. This in itself was a most remarkable thing, for the State Church had before refused to fraternize with the Free Church. But all had come to listen to a new Farel of this nineteenth century. As Farel roused that city by his eloquence to become Protestant in the days of the Reformation, so Lacroix roused them to become missionaries in spirit by his eloquence, and a new era began to dawn on the churches of the French cantons. With all the eloquence which had made him in India the best preacher in Bengali, he now pleads with his Swiss friends to interest themselves in missions. And at the close of his lecture, with a voice broken with deep emotion, he bade them farewell. The collection for Foreign Missions that day in the boxes at the door of the church amounted to one hundred and sixty dollars, an amount unheard of before.

Nor did the influence of these lectures end then. For the next day, as he was making a farewell call at Professor Munier's, a lady had a chance meeting with him, which had a marked influence on his after life. She had been deeply impressed with his lecture of the day before, so that she said at the close of his lecture: "Now we *must* do something." At Professor Munier's house she offered to give four hundred dollars, a very large sum then, and she started a movement that raised five thousand dollars for his work before he died, through the societies which she organized. All these results came from her words: "We must do something." His eloquent lectures on missions Lacroix repeated at Lausanne and at Neuchatel, and later at Brussels and Paris. Everywhere they were heard with profound attention and deep interest. The Paris Missionary Society was so pleased with them that they sent in a request to the London Missionary Society to allow Mr. Lacroix to remain in Europe for another year, so as to lecture throughout France and rouse interest in missions. The London Society, however, felt itself compelled to refuse the request, as he was greatly needed in India. His missionary work in Switzerland was, however, only second to his missionary work in India in importance. It disarmed prejudice and awakened interest. It started an influence which led, many years later, to the founding, in 1874, of the Foreign Missionary Society of the French churches of Switzerland, which is now doing such an admirable work in Southern Africa.

He returned to India in 1844, to take up the work he so much loved. But he did not find his work as hopeful as it had been during the years before. The first love and zeal in many of his converts had passed away. In 1854 there was a relapse. On one occasion he suspended the communion at Rammakalchoke for a whole year, while the Gungree church was entirely broken up. Still from these churches more than two hundred in thirty years at last found their home in heaven. In spite of these difficulties he labored on. He retained his deep interest in the missionary societies at home, and when the Revolution of 1848 bankrupted the Paris Missionary Society, he so plead for their successful mission among the Basutos that he was able to secure four thousand dollars for them in India. This aid, with the money raised for them in southern Africa, enabled that society to continue its work, until in a year or two it was able to recover itself.

He thus describes an impressive scene in his tours: "In the afternoon we proceeded to the village of the Kamarjani Proper, in doing which we had to cross a small but rapid river. The weekly market was just being held, and the crowd of buyers and sellers was most dense, not less than three thousand persons being present. We found it very difficult to make our way through the mass of human beings, and having at last reached a spot a little clearer than the rest, we made a halt. Mr. Hill then read part of a tract, at which we were surrounded by many hundreds and so hemmed in that we had scarcely elbow room. Then I made an address, and it required the highest power of my voice to make myself heard by all. I told them that this was a happy day for their village, for I had come to announce to them the true incarnation, the incarnation of mercy, that Jesus Christ had come into the world to save men from sin and hell, and to open the gates of heaven to all who repent and believe on Him. The attention was intense, and repeated exclamations of surprise and wonder were uttered at this news, which for the first time came to their ears. The people never having seen Christian missionaries, gave vent to various surmises as to who we might be. The prevailing opinion was that we were of the oldest and more reverend Brahminical race in the northwest of India. 'Look at them!' says one. "How resplendent their countenances are and what fire proceeds from their mouths when they speak, the very marks of the real original Brahminical race.'

"The sermon was followed by an unusual demand for tracts and books, which it was difficult to supply. Finding it was impossible to speak any longer, I told the assembled crowd that we were servants of Jesus Christ, of whom they had just heard, and that we brought books with us, which would explain more fully all that had been done for the salvation of men. On this the rush was so general that we dared not attempt distribution, and walked to a more distant spot. But being followed by the whole of our audience, we were equally unsuccessful. In four different places we tried to persuade them to sit down, so that we might distribute the books with some regularity, but it was in vain. For the outer rows, fearing the books would be expended before their turn came, rose and came falling upon those before them, until the confusion became so great that a lad was thrown down by the crowd, and would have been trampled to death, if Mr. Hill had not seized him by the hair and extricated him from his perilous position. We therefore went to a place near by, a mile from the market, when we found the number of our applicants reduced about one hundred, where we distributed the books. Never elsewhere in India did I see such eagerness to obtain books as was displayed on this occasion."

For seven years after his return from Europe he acted as pastor, but after 1851 he was set free from pastoral work, so that he might spend his whole time in preaching. In 1851 the school, which he had so successfully started in Calcutta, was enlarged, and exerted a wide influence among the Hindus. Thus in preaching, pastoral work and education, nearly forty years passed away in India. His strong form gradually became weakened by age and enfeebled by disease. He was temporarily supplying the English chapel, when on May 19, 1859, he was suddenly taken ill with his old affection of the liver. In India diseases are few, but when they come, they are deadly and quick. His Christian friends soon became alarmed about his condition, and a daily prayer meeting was held to pray for him. One minister in them, referring to him, said, "Who ever thinks of Mr. Lacroix as belonging to the London Missionary Society? He belongs to us all." Lacroix's prayer in the midst of his great suffering was: "O Lord, counterbalance by Thy presence the pain which I now feel." He dwelt continually in his thoughts on God's presence. One day a member of the family was about to repeat some amusing remark just made by one of his grandchildren, when he said: "No; don't tell me. Speak to me only of heavenly things." Two weeks of suffering passed away. when, July 2, he suddenly grew worse. His nephew, Dr. Vos, felt it right to inform him that his end was approaching. "So much the better," he replied. Often his mind wandered through the disease, but his friends had only to speak the name of Jesus, and at once a heavenly smile broke over his wasted face. "His interviews in his sickness with missionaries of all denominations," says one, "were most affecting; and his love to them and theirs for him is best illustrated by Paul's farewell at Miletus." He fell asleep in Jesus on the eighth of July, 1859. A great company followed him to his grave, including the Episcopal Bishop of Calcutta. The native Christians carried the coffin from the hearse to the grave. And a few days after, Rev. Dr. Duff preached to one of the largest congregations ever gathered in Calcutta on such an occasion, on "Know ye not that there is a prince and a great man fallen this day in Israel?"

Lacroix was a remarkable man in many ways. In addition to his remarkable ability as a preacher, he excelled as a linguist. He could preach well in five languages before he was twenty-six years of age.

The distinguishing characteristics of his disposition were his exceeding amiability and sound sense.

Next to William Carey, says Smith the historian of India missions, was Lacroix as a preacher to the Bengali in their native tongue. The epitaph on his tomb is: "As a preacher to the heathen he excelled, as a pastor he was greatly beloved, as a man of undoubted integrity, wisdom and benevolence he was implicitly trusted, as a Christian he was universally honored."

Chapter II.

JOHN SCUDDER.

One of the saints among modern missionaries was Rev. John Scudder, for thirty-six years missionary to India. The universal respect in which he was held by all with whom he came in contact, reveals his high spiritual power as a missionary. Rev. J. L. Phillips, secretary of the Sunday-school work in India, says of him: "He was one of the most godly men I ever met." He was also a surgeon—like Luke, a beloved physician—but also like Paul, an evangelistic missionary.

He was born at Freehold, New Jersey, on September 3, 1793. He very early showed traits of missionary activity. Some missionaries are born, others are made—made so by the grace of God. He was a born missionary; for from his early childhood he showed the missionary spirit. One day he was found drawing a very heavy rail, and was asked what he expected to do with it. His reply was: "I am taking it to Miss Becky, who has no fire." Indeed, he was accustomed to gather sticks, in order to kindle the fires of the destitute. There was a neighbor, a drunkard, who abused his wife, even driving her from home at midnight, so that she had to seek shelter in her father's house. One day John, who frequently went to him, said to him: "Why do they call you 'Devil John?'" The man's wife was very much frightened, as she was afraid her husband would hurt John for asking such a question. Then John asked him: "If you will throw away your bottle, I will keep Lent with your wife" (for she was an Episcopalian). Strange to say, the man assented. John's words were a message of God to him. The man then became an abstainer, and joined the church. And long after, when John was a missionary in India, he sent a message to the old man: "I charge you to meet me in heaven," which very much affected him.

He then attended Princeton College, but, unlike some students, he did not forget his Christian character while there. The direct opposite was true, for he was always on the lookout for souls. Although infidelity ruled the colleges in his day, and only three out of the one hundred and twenty students at Princeton were professing Christians, yet he labored as a Christian among the students. He was rated by others as "so religious that they dared hardly laugh in his presence." But that very remark led another student to seek his companionship, whom he soon after brought to the Saviour. For when Scudder found he was serious, he took him on a walk to the woods, and there led him to give himself up to Christ in prayer. Having graduated, 1811, he studied medicine at the College of Physicians and Surgeons in New York City, and then located there.

As yet missions were little known, or this born missionary would have naturally gravitated toward them. But he became a missionary physician, often leading his patients to a greater Physician than himself. He early sought a church home, and found it in the Reformed Dutch church on Franklin street, of which Rev. Mr. Bork was pastor. (Mr. Bork had been a Hessian soldier from Germany, and had been converted in this country through Rev. Dr. Livingston's preaching in a barn.) Dr. Scudder did not rest until in the family where he boarded, the mother, two daughters and one son were brought into the Church. But sometimes his experiences were sad as well as glad. He was called one day to see a sick girl in one of the tenements. He took a friend along, who tells the story. The young girl was beautiful with the paleness of death. And yet she groaned—and such a groan. The doctor spoke to her tenderly about Jesus. But her look showed that to her that name was agony. She cried out: "Pray for me—I am lost." They knelt and prayed, weeping as they did so. She would break out, while they prayed, with exclamations, "Pray on; don't stop; O I am lost!" Soon her spasms stopped their prayers, and with an awful groan she passed away.

We now come to his call to become a missionary. How strangely God calls the attention of men to the mission field. How often a book does it. "Brainerd's Diary" led Carey to go to India. And the "Star of the East," by Buchanan, led Judson to Burmah. So, too, one day when Scudder was visiting a Christian patient, he found on a table in her room a book, whose title at once attracted his attention, "The Conversion of the World, or the Claims of Six Hundred Millions." He borrowed the book, read it, and reread it. It was a Macedonian cry to him. He fell on his knees, asking, like Paul: "Lord, what wilt thou have me to do?" God answered in calling him to a foreign land. He then anxiously and prayerfully announced to his wife his decision. Nobly she answered like Ruth: "Whither thou goest, I will go." But many of his associates thought otherwise, some even, like Festus with Paul,

The Reformed Church. 193

thinking that he was mad for giving up his fine practice and throwing himself away on the heathen. But his decision being once made, he never flinched.

He applied to the American Board to know whether they would send a physician. How wonderful are the cross purposes of Providence. A call comes from one end of the earth, and at the same time its answer from the other. It happened that just as he offered himself the American Board was asked for a physician in India who could practice medicine as well as preach. They gladly accepted his offer, and arrangements were made for him to sail from Boston. Now the sailing of a missionary in those days, being much less common than today, was a remarkable event. On June 8, 1819, a large company gathered to see him off. Some looked upon him as going to bury himself alive. Yet his face shone so radiant with hope that it left a deep impression on all who were present. Among those present was James Brainerd Taylor, who from that moment devoted himself to Christ. Taylor said: "What is it that lifts this missionary into the precincts of heaven? Surely he is possessed with the spirit and temper of his Master." Young Taylor went to his home so deeply impressed that he could not return to business. He retired into prayer, and soon after left business for Christian work; and after most remarkable labors for Christ, went home to his reward at the age of twenty.

Dr. Scudder was now on board the brig "Indus," bound for Calcutta. He had as companions three other missionaries. It was a long journey of many months. He did not wait until he arrived in India before he began his missionary work. As he had been a missionary at home, he now became a missionary on shipboard. He began distributing Bibles and tracts among the sailors. It soon became evident that some of them, in the loneliness of the voyage, were reading them. About two weeks after they sailed, one of the sailors fell overboard and came very near losing his life. That evening Dr. Scudder, with two of the other missionaries, went forward among them and impressed on them the importance of preparing for death.

Soon the fruits began to appear. Strange to say, the first was one of the most hardened, as he had ridiculed religion when he came on board. But on the evening when the missionaries spoke to them about the sailor who fell overboard, this man became impressed and determined to break off from his sins. But as he was an infidel, and had sneered at the "holy brotherhood," as he called the missionaries when they came aboard, he now had to pass through the deepest struggles of conviction before he found Christ. The next to submit was a young man who, too, had ridiculed the missionaries. He began reading a Bible they gave him, but finding its way of salvation too hard, he gave up reading it and took up "Baxter's Saints' Rest," hoping to find in it an easier way to heaven. He soon found, however, that it taught just what the Bible did. He was finally brought to Christ through reading the "Life of John Newton." These two were the first fruits—the harbingers of greater blessings yet to come.

Suddenly, when they had been out at sea three months, the Spirit of God came down upon them like a wind, and within a week there was not a thoughtless sinner aboard. This was one of the most remarkable awakenings ever known on shipboard. There was no excitement connected with it. It did not come as the result of a series of meetings, for five of those convicted of sin were alone when convicted. The very silence of the movement made it the more impressive. The first mate, who had ridiculed religion and was a Universalist, while in the act of having the harpoon raised to strike a fish, was struck with the arrow of conviction. He became so humbled with his guilt that "he felt," he said, "below the dog they had on board." Then it was the second mate's turn. (It looked as if God was calling the ship's roll for converts.) While up in the rigging, the Spirit of God, stronger than the wind then blowing, convicted him, and after a terrible struggle with darling sins, he soon rejoiced in Christ, and even longed to be ridiculed for Christ, as he had once ridiculed Christians.

Perhaps the most remarkable trophy was the cook, one of the most profane men aboard. He happened to overhear two of the sailors talking about the Holy Spirit's work, and said in fun, "May God grant that the Spirit of God may light on every soul on board." That night what he said in fun came to him in awful earnest. The Holy Spirit terribly convicted him of sin, and soon, from being a cross, morose man, he became pleasant and obliging, because Christ had found him. A man by the name of Parker, who was so profane that, as he said, he "blasphemed enough to damn a thousand souls," swore at the captain for urging them to become better. But the blasphemer, too, became a follower of

Christ. Thus the Spirit went from man to man, converting the steward, the carpenter and others by His power. It was a modern Pentecost—a foretaste of heaven. At length, after this blessed season of grace, they at last arrived at Calcutta.

When Mr. Scudder arrived in India, he located in that paradise of earth, Ceylon, whose spicy breezes are fragrant many miles out at sea, where

> "Every prospect pleases
> And only man is vile."

He located at Panditeripo, in July, 1820. Here he began his work as a preacher and a physician. Many came to him for medicine, and as he healed their bodies, Christ through him healed their souls. In 1821 he was ordained there to the ministry. There were also missionary schools for boys and girls at Panditeripo and in the neighborhood. These Mrs. Scudder took charge of, while he went out to hospital practice or else on preaching tours through the villages. God's Spirit soon showed Himself, especially in the schools, as now and then a boy or girl united with the Church. These, however, were only the first-fruits, the harbingers of the coming harvest. For after he had been at work there for four years, a modern Pentecost took place. We will let his wife describe it, by giving extracts from her letters.

She says: "The evening of February 12, 1824, will ever be a memorable night to us. On that day we went to Baticalo in the afternoon to converse with the boys in that school. A meeting was held with our boys in the evening before we went. After the meeting, it being moonlight, many of the boys were engaged in playing. They left their play and began spreading their mats upon which they sleep. Amy (the servant) told Whelpley to go to the children and talk to them about their souls. He accordingly went to them, spoke a few words and then left them. Very soon the voice of prayer was heard in the garden. This increased until from every part of the garden was heard the cry: 'What shall I do to be saved?' When we returned home from Baticalo, the doors and windows were all open, the moon shining brightly, and our servant was weeping on the veranda. The heart-rending cry was heard from every part of the garden: 'To whom shall I go?' 'Have mercy on me, Lord Jesus.' 'O give me Thy Holy Spirit.' 'I have been a great sinner,' and many more expressions of great earnestness, which seemed to proceed from broken hearts of sin.

"After learning that they had been in this affecting way, crying for mercy more than an hour, the Doctor thought it prudent to ring the bell and call them to the house. They came with tears streaming down their cheeks. Upon looking round upon the precious flock, we found them to be twenty-nine in number—all in the school except four. We conversed and prayed with them. In the afternoon of that day the Doctor had sent word to the boys for those who were willing to forsake all for Christ to come to him. Sixteen came. One proud boy said he would not give up all for Christ; but in the evening it would have melted a heart of stone to have seen that boy bowed down like a bulrush and scarcely able to speak for sobs and tears. As a result of this remarkable awakening in the mission station, forty-one were admitted to the Church; and although thirty of the scholars desired to join the Church, only half were admitted because of the violent opposition they would have to suffer from the heathen around."

After this glorious awakening Dr. Scudder continued in Ceylon till 1836, when it was deemed wise that he should change his residence to Madras in India. In this large city he labored, as he had done in Ceylon, with great faithfulness and success. He sometimes suffered insult in his missionary journeys. Several times he was stoned. His journey through the jungle in 1841 was a record of danger and sacrifice. But God protected him from wild beasts and wild men, until jungle fever laid him low. When he had recovered, 1842, he was ordered back to America to recuperate. He spent about three years in his native land. When asked in America what were the discouragements of missionary work, he replied: "I do not know the word. I long ago erased it from my vocabulary." He was greater than Napoleon who ruled the word "impossible" out of his dictionary, saying it was the language of fools. Dr. Scudder's "discouragements" were only encouragements to greater work. But although in a Christian land, he did the work of a missionary. He went about everywhere, stirring up the churches to missionary activity. During that time he traveled from Maine to Georgia, and addressed, it is said, 100,000 children and youth upon the subject of missions.

His success among the children was very remarkable. The diaries of many of them related that "Dr. Scudder of India asked me this day if I would not give my heart to Jesus, and if I grew up I would be a missionary and come to India." And many years after, when these children had grown up, the secretary of the Mission Board bore testimony to the results of his tour—that the applicants for missionary work, when asked what led them to think of missions, would often reply: "Dr. Scudder's addresses and appeals to me when I was a child." His ministry at home was therefore as successful as his ministry among the heathen. But he was glad to return to India, for he said: "There is no place like India; it is nearer heaven than America."

He returned in 1846 to do a good work at Madura and then at Madras. On one of his tours an immense crowd collected together. A band of fierce Musselmen demanded books of his helper, who carried the tracts. When he refused, one of them advanced, brandishing a club, with which he, supported by his angry companions, would no doubt have killed him and Dr. Scudder; but the latter, with admirable self-possession, ran up to the enemy, and stroking his beard, exclaimed: "My brother, my brother!" This token of Oriental obeisance appeased him, and the missionary's life was spared. Dr. Scudder confessed afterward that he felt the danger so imminent that the saliva dried up in his mouth as if parched by long thirst. But his excessive labors, aided by bereavements, again broke him down, and he went to the Cape of Good Hope in South Africa to recuperate. Here, worn out as he was, he again began a campaign for missions, such as had been so successful in America. But just before a public meeting he laid down to rest and suddenly fell asleep in Jesus January 13, 1855. Thus ended a life of remarkable success. Dr. Scudder was one of the first medical missionaries and one of the ablest. He was a man of rare tact and noble courage. But above all shone the rare spirituality of his character and his devotion to Christ. Two and a half hours of every day were set apart for meditation and prayer. Every Friday till midday was spent in fasting and prayer. He walked constantly with God, and like Enoch, he was not, for God took him.

"No stronger, more versatile or more successful missionary pioneer ever evangelized a people as healer, preacher, teacher and translator," says Smith the historian of Indian Missions. He lived in praying and working till, although he knew it not, he realized his ambition in this world, "to be one of the inner circle around Jesus." His descendants to the fourth generation became missionaries. Of his son Silas he said, "Make him a Christian," and "Make him a missionary." But the son resisted, determined to make a fortune as a physician in New York City where he founded a woman's hospital. But he was powerless against his father's prayers, and went as a medical missionary to Arcot, India, where his institution was the admiration of the governor of Madras and English noblemen. The Scudder family has given thirty persons to the cause of missions, and up to 1896 their united labors represented 529 years for India. There was not a town in southeast India that had not heard the gospel from his lips, not a village that his Tamil publications did not penetrate.

Chapter III.
JACOB CHAMBERLAIN.

One of the greatest living missionaries is Rev. Jacob Chamberlain, of Southern India. He was born at Sharon, Connecticut, April 18, 1835. He graduated at Western Reserve College in 1856, and at the New Brunswick Theological Seminary in 1859. In that year he sailed for India under the appointment of the Dutch Board, having taken a course in medicine at the College of Physicians and Surgeons at New York City, and also at the Cleveland Medical College. He was one of the early medical missionaries, but found it an exceedingly great help to him in his evangelistic tours. When he entered the Arcot mission in India, 1859, he learned the Tamil language as he expected to labor among the Tamils. But he was transferred (1863) to a district which spoke the Telugu language. So his life has been spent in working among them since 1863, making his centre at Mardanapalle, one hundred and fifty miles inland from Madras. There he did a large work in a large field, his territory being as large as the whole of the State of Connecticut. For many years he was the only physician in that area. Before he returned home in 1874, that is in fifteen years, he had personally treated 30,000 patients.

His literary labors are shown by the fact that he was chairman of a committee of all the missions who labored among the Telugus, and who aimed to produce a translation of the Bible in that language which is spoken by eighteen millions. In 1863 he made an extended missionary tour of four months, going northward through the countries of the Nizam of Hyderabad and of the Ghronis and Kios who had never seen a missionary. He thus describes some of the scenes:

"On a certain occasion I went into a native city in India, where the name of Jesus had never been heard, to preach for them Jesus and his salvation and to scatter among them His Word. As an introduction we had assembled an audience in the street. I asked my native assistant to read the first chapter of Romans—that chapter which those (in Christian lands) who call themselves too liberal-minded, tell us is too black to be true—a libel on human nature. That chapter was read. The most intelligent man in the audience, a Brahmin, stepped forward and said to me: 'Sir, that chapter must have been written for us Hindus. It describes us exactly.' What a proof that Scripture was written by the Holy Spirit who searcheth the hearts of men just as he does the deep things of God."

"On another occasion I went into a city where Jesus had never been proclaimed. As we passed up the street I noticed a small Hindoo temple built upon the side of the busiest street with its doors open and idols at the farther end so that passers-by could worship as they went. At the side of the door sat a Brahmin priest to receive the worship and gifts of the people passing by. Going up the street and finding no better place I returned to this temple and asked permission to speak from its steps. The Brahmin gave it politely. Singing a song to bring the people together, we soon had the street packed. I took for my theme the character of the Being whom an intelligent person would like to worship as God. I attempted to show that he must be stronger than ourselves; omnipotent (that we can trust him) omniscient, omnipresent, a God of love, justice, etc. I painted the picture of our God without telling them where He could be found. The intelligent men said: 'Yes; my picture was true.' I then asked: 'Who is God and where is He? The Brahmin priest, suspecting my object was to undermine his faith, tried to divert the people. He straightened himself up and drew his finger across his stomach saying: 'Sir, this is my god; when this is full my god is propitious; when this is empty my god is angry. Only give me enough to eat and drink and that is all the god I want.' I turned and reminded the bystanders of the pure God I had been describing and then by way of contrast, I pointed them to his god. He slank away amid their sneers and vanished down a side street. How the audience listened when I described our God incarnate in Jesus."

He passed through many perils which he most vividly describes and applies in his tracts and his two books "In the Tiger Jungle" and "The Cobra's Den." He is an inimitable story teller, bringing home the religious application with telling power. He thus describes a hair-breadth escape on this tour:

"I wish you could have witnessed a scene in the kingdom of Hyderabad. There, in a city—a walled town, of about 18,000 inhabitants, the people had arisen to drive us out, because we tried to speak of another God than theirs. We had gone into the market place, and I had endeavored to preach to them of Christ and His salvation but they would not hear. They ordered us to leave the city at once, but I had declined to leave until I had delivered to them my message. The throng was filling the streets. They told me if I tried to utter another word I should be killed. There was no rescue. They would have the city gates closed and there would never any news go forth of what was done. I must leave that city at once or I would not leave it alive. I had seen them tear up the paving stones and fill their arms with them so as to be ready. And one of them was saying to another: 'You throw the first stone and I will throw the next.' By an artifice I need not stop to detail I succeeded in getting permission to tell them a story before they stoned me and then they might stone me if they wished. I told them the story of all stories—of the love of the Divine Father that had made us all of one blood, who so loved the world that he gave His only begotten Son. I told the story of that birth in the manger at Bethlehem, of that wonderful childhood, of that marvelous life, of those miraculous deeds, of the gracious words He spoke. I told them the story of the cross and pictured in graphic words, that the Master gave me that day, the story of the Saviour nailed upon the cross for them, for me, for all the world, when he cried out in agony: 'My God, my God, why hast thou forsaken me.' When I told them that, I saw the men go and throw their stones into the gutter and come back, and down the cheeks of the very men that had been clamoring the loudest for my blood I saw the tears running and dropping on the pavement they had torn up. And then I told them how he had been laid in the grave and how after three days He had come forth triumphant and had ascended again to heaven and that there He ever lives to make intercession for us, for them, for all the world, and that through His words every one of them might receive remission of sins and eternal life. I told them I had finished my story and they might stone me now. But no, they did not want to stone me now. They did not know what a wonderful story I had come to tell them. They came forward and bought Scriptures and Gospels and tracts and paid money for them, for they wanted to know more of that wonderful Saviour of whom I had told them." He then adds one of his apt applications: "Brother minister, we can not find anything better than the old, old story to proclaim. Let us do our work under the original commission of Christ—'Preach the gospel to every creature.' Then we shall succeed."

Another very remarkable story in his life was his escape in answer to prayer. On this tour he found himself overtaken by the rainy season and on the outskirts of the jungle, where the ground was covered with water and where lurked fever and man-eating tigers. He applied to the governor for forty coolies or bearers. And the governor furnished a guard over them so that they would not run away. But alas, they had not gone far before both coolies and guard vanished rather than face the terrors of the jungle at that season. He proceeded as best he could to the next station where he demanded assistance. The governor said: "No." But Dr. Chamberlain produced the firman of the government compelling every one, under severe penalties if he refused, to assist him. The governor secured forty coolies and Dr. Chamberlain paid them in advance so as to insure their staying and watched them so that they did not desert. His objective point was a cataract sixty miles away where they expected to find a boat on which they could float down the river. Above the cataract a boat could not be found and the river had overflowed its banks. All day they waded in the jungle under the alternations of heavy showers and boiling, sickening sun. Toward evening they met two hunters returning and running if possible to reach the highlands before dark, as they were afraid of the wild beasts of the jungle at night. They told Dr. Chamberlain that there was not a hill or a hillock where he could pitch a tent for the night, nothing but water endlessly stretched out like what they had been splashing through all day. Must he and his band perish? He said that in his extremity he prayed while on horseback to his covenant God: "O Lord, I am helpless to extricate myself from this dangerous situation. Yet I am thy servant and in obedience to the command of the Lord Jesus have come to India to preach the gospel to the heathen. In His service I have been brought into this difficulty and peril. Be pleased to show me where I can go." Immediately an answer came as distinctly pronounced in his ear as ever words were spoken in the ears of anybody: "Turn to the left, go down the river and you will find what you need." Immediately he conferred with his guides who assured him of the folly of proceeding in that direction. Then came the voice again repeating the direction first given. Consulting with his guides again he was told that the river had overflowed its banks and it was impossible that a rescue could come from that direction. For the third time the voice came, "Turn to the left, proceed to the river and you will find what you want." Then as master of the company he gave the order to turn to the left and coming to the river—what did he see? The very thing he needed most, a large flat boat and in it two boatmen. They, mistaking him for an English officer, began to apologize for the boat's appearance at so strange a spot. They said the flood in the river had loosened the boat from its moorings, and that "the devil himself seemed to be in that boat," for despite all their efforts to the contrary it persisted in floating to the spot where it was found by Dr. Chamberlain. Armed as he was with the authority of the British government, he took possession of it, and found it just broad enough to allow the spreading of his tent, under which he slept undisturbed by the hungry tigers whom he heard howling in the jungle. It was not the devil that was in that boat as they blasphemously declared, but the Lord was in it, causing it to come to the rescue of his missionary.

The next morning they continued floating down the river until they came to the next cataract where he found another boat and relief from all anxiety. This was a most remarkable answer to prayer.

Nowhere is he more happy than in his tracts based on some incident in his life or in India. His most famous tract has been the one entitled "Winding up a Horse." Its influence has been so great that it has brought, it is said, $30,000 into the treasury of the Dutch Reformed Foreign Board. He says:

"Nineteen years ago (1860) I bought in Madras a peculiar kind of horse. He had to be wound up to make him go.

It was not a machine, but a veritable live horse. When breaking him to go in the carriage he had been injured. An accident occurred in starting him the first time, and he was thrown and hurt and frightened. It made him timid; afraid to start. After he had once started he would not balk, until taken out of the carriage. He would start and stop and go on as many times as you pleased, but it was very difficult to get him started at first each time he was harnessed to the carriage.

He was all right under the saddle, an excellent riding horse, and would carry me long distances in my district work, so that I did not wish to dispose of him, but I could not afford to keep two. Whatever I had must go in carriage as well as ride, and I determined that I would conquer.

How I have worked over that horse! At first it sometimes took me an hour to get him started from my door. At last, after trying everything I had ever heard of, I hit upon an expedient that worked.

I took a strong bamboo stick two feet long and over an inch thick. A stout cord loop was passed through a hole two inches from its end. This loop we would slip over his left ear down to the roots, and turn the stick 'round and 'round and twist it up.

It is said that a horse can retain but one idea at a time in its small brain. Soon the twisting would begin to hurt. His attention would be attracted to the pain in his ear. He would forget all about a carriage being hitched to him, bend down his head and walk off as quiet as a lamb. When he had gone a rod the horse boy would begin to untwist; soon off would come the cord, and the horse would be all right for the day. The remedy never failed.

After having it on two or three times, he objected to the operation, and would spring about and rear and twitch and back, anything but start ahead, to keep it from being applied. We would have two of us, to begin to pat and rub about his neck and head. He would not know which had the key. All at once it would be on his ear and winding up. The moment it began to tighten he would be quiet, stand and bear it as long as he could, and then off he would go.

It never took thirty seconds to get him off with the key. It would take an hour without. After a little he ceased objecting to have it put on. He seemed to say to himself: "I have got to give in and may as well do it at once," but he would not start without the key. In a few months he got so that, as soon as we got into the carriage, he would bend down his head to have the key put on, and one or two turns of the key would be enough.

Then the key became unnecessary. He would bend down his head, tipping his left ear to the horse boy, who would take it in his hand and twist it and off he would go.

My native neighbors said, "That horse must be wound up or he cannot run." And it seemed to be so.

When he got so that the "winding up" was nothing but a form, I tried to break him of that, but could not succeed. I would pat him and talk to him and give him a little salt or sugar or bread, and then step quietly into the carriage and tell him to go. "No." Coax him. "No." Whip him. "No."

Legs braced, every muscle tense for resistance. A genuine balk. Stop and keep quiet for an instant, and he would hold down his head, bend over his ear and look around for the horse boy appealingly, saying very earnestly by his actions: "Do please wind me up. I can't go without, but I'll gladly if you will." The moment his ear was touched and one twist given, off he would go as happy and contented as ever horse could be.

Many hearty laughs have we and our friends had over the winding up of that horse. If I were out on a tour for a month or two, and he was not hitched to the carriage, or if he stood in the stable with no work for a week or two during the monsoon, a real winding up had to take place the first time he was put in. We kept him six years. The last week I owned him I had to wind him up. I sold the patent with the horse, and learned from the man that bought him that he had to use it as long as the horse lived.

I was thinking about that horse the other night when it was too hot to sleep, and I suddenly burst into a laugh as I said to myself: "I have again and again, in the membership of our churches at home, seen the horse that had to be wound up, in all matters of benevolence."

Another very popular tract of Dr. Chamberlain is entitled "Break Cocoanuts over the Wheels." He says:

"It was twenty years ago. We had recently located in the heathen town of Madanapalle, India, to commence missionary work there.

The time for the annual drawing of the great idol car through the streets of the town and by the banks of the river had come. Multitudes of votaries from all the villages around, as well as from every street of the town, had assembled before the car. Great rope cables were attached. Hundreds caught hold of the ropes. Up went the shout: "Hari! Hari! Háyi! Jayam!" "Vishnu! Vishnu! Joy and Victory!" "Now pull," shouted the priests, and off went the three-storied car majestically through the streets, amid the joyous shouts of the thousands of spectators. On they followed it to the river bank. Libations were brought and poured over the car, and the multitudinous ceremonies performed.

Again, with similar shouts, they began the progress around by different streets, back to the great temple before which the car always reposed for the year. Half way back and the car came to a stand. "Pull," shouted the priests. Pull they did. The ropes snapped with the strain. All the wheels were examined; no stones were in the way; everything seemed right. The ropes were tied and new ones added. More votaries caught the ropes. "All pull," shouted the priests. All bent to the effort. It would not move.

A pallor came over the crowd. "The god is angry and will not let his chariot move," was whispered along the streets. A feeling of dread shivered through the multitude. "Yes," shouted the chief priest from the car, "the god is angry. He will not move unless you propitiate him. Run all of you and bring cocoanuts and break over the wheels, and as the fragrant cocoanut milk runs down over the wheels the god will accept the libation and graciously allow his chariot to move on again. Run, and each bring a cocoanut! Run!"

Men and boys ran for the cocoanuts; the residents to their houses, the villagers to the bazaars to buy or to their friends' houses to borrow. Each came back with his cocoanut, and broke it over one of the wheels. The cocoanut milk ran along the streets. "Háyi! Jayam," shouted the priests. "The god is now propitious." "Háyi! Jayam!" "Joy! Victory!" shouted the multitude. "Now pull all!"

shouted the priests. The people took heart; dread passed away; confidence came. They seized the ropes and, with a shout that resounded in the hills a mile away, they gave a pull. Off went the car, and soon, with singing and dancing, they had it back in its wonted place. And as the crowd scattered to their village homes, the news ran through the country: "The car got set; they could not move it a finger breadth; but each man brought a cocoanut and broke it over the wheels, and then on it went with a rush to the temple."

This scene flashes upon my memory as I read the appeals of all the missions for enlargement answered by the "empty treasuries" of the Missionary Boards.

God's chariot is delayed. His Chariot of Salvation had started in its course in towns in India and China and Japan through the agency of the Reformed Church. Have the people lost heart that it stands still? Has discouragement come upon us?

"Run for cocoanuts." Let each man and boy, let each woman and each child bring what would be to them the equivalent in value of a cocoanut to the poor Hindu, as an offering to the Lord, and the chariot will move joyously on."

Others of his inimitable tracts might be given but

space forbids. The reader is referred to his books, "The Tiger Jungle" and "In the Cobra's Den," for other stories equally good. These books ought to be in every Sunday-school library.

Dr. Chamberlain still continues his work in southern India. He was one of the most prominent missionaries at the Ecumenical Conference of Missions at New York City in 1900. Although his health has failed him, yet he still delights to tell the sweet story of Jesus, and to preach the precious doctrines of our Heidelberg Catechism.

The Arcot Mission of the Dutch Reformed Church in India, has been greatly blessed. It reports in 1901, 2,442 communicants in 24 churches, and 157 outstations; 167 Sunday-schools with 5,406 scholars.

D. Abeel

B.—China.

Chapter IV.

DAVID ABEEL.

Rev. David Abeel was one of the pioneer missionaries of the Dutch Reformed Church of America. He was born June 12, 1804, at New Brunswick, New Jersey, of parents who emigrated to America from Amsterdam. When fifteen years of age, he made application to the West Point Military Academy, but owing to the great number of applicants, he was induced to withdraw his request. Providence had, unknown to himself, determined that he should be a soldier in a higher service than that of the United States. He then turned his attention to medicine, and while engaged in its study, came under deep religious conviction. Many weary days and sleepless nights were his, as he struggled on to the light. Finally, under the wise counsels of Rev. Dr. Livingston, he found Christ, and then the great question of his life became: "How can I do the most for the Master?" In 1823 he entered the theological seminary at New Brunswick, remaining there three years. During that time he was busy in mission work. While in seminary he wrote down the following resolution: "Conscious of the importance of making an unreserved surrender of myself to the service of Him under whose banner I have enlisted, I would solemnly determine, by the restraining influence of the Spirit of God, on this, the 15th of September, 1825, to renounce every known sin, though it cost me the pain of plucking out an eye or cutting off a hand, and of living as far as possible a life consistent with my high vocation." On April 20, 1826, he was licensed to preach, at which time he wrote: "I feel impressed with the view of the solemnity and deep responsibility of my office. My life, my health, my time, my talents, all that I have, I sincerely desire to consecrate to his service. And now would I come to the determination in my Father's strength to live a life of faith and holiness—to keep myself unspotted from the world—to live in the habitual commission of no sin—to mortify the old man with his affections and lusts. Oh, how shall I preach to others that which I practice not myself? O Thou, great God, I have no strength of my own; I look to Thee for Thy grace."

He was called that year as pastor of the Reformed church at Athens, New York. He describes the place as being in morals very much like its namesake in the old world. But he bravely began his work, at first in a school house, as the congregation had no church of their own. Earnestly he prayed for the outpouring of God's Spirit, and the Lord blessed his two and a half years' ministry there to the salvation of many souls. His incessant labors, however, broke down a frame never very strong, and he was forced to leave. Meanwhile he had been reading missionary works, as the lives of Brainerd and Martyn. These prepared him to make his ultimate choice for missions. Two main difficulties lay in his way. One was his own feeble health, the other was the fact that he was the only son of his parents, and they were slow to give their consent. Just then, however, Providence opened the way, for the Seaman's Friend Society wanted some one to go to Canton, in China, to preach to the sailors there, and the American Board wanted him to prepare to preach to the Chinese. Hoping that a sea voyage would build up his health, and that he would get an opportunity to preach the gospel to the heathen, he sailed, October 14, 1829, and reached Canton February 25, 1830.

He at once began to work very faithfully among

the seamen, but after laboring thus for the Seaman's Friend Society for nearly a year, he was transferred to the American Board for whose work he had been preparing by spending much time in learning the Chinese language. Yet it was dangerous to study Chinese. When the Chinese teacher was instructing him, he kept his door locked. When the officers came to see what the foreigners were doing, the teacher put the books in a box and material for making shoes on the top, as he feared he might lose his head if it were found out that he taught the foreigners Chinese. As Abeel could do nothing in China because foreigners were not allowed to teach Christianity, the American Board ordered him to make a tour of the islands of the Archipelago and visit Java, Borneo, Siam and the Dutch missions there that he might labor among the Chinese scattered in those islands.

During these voyages he distributed Christian books, held religious conversation with the sailors and with the Chinese. While at Batavia, he stayed with the earnest missionary, Mr. Medhurst, and engaged with him in mission work, and also in the study of the Chinese language.

His health failing, in 1833 he was compelled to

come to America. During the voyage his health greatly improved. He landed in 1833 first in England, where his physicians urged him not to sail to America during the winter. He then went to Paris, where he stirred up interest in missions by holding missionary meetings. When he returned to England July 25, 1834, he described the degradations of the women of the East. He showed that missionaries' wives who had always done what they could, were unable on account of family duties to do all that was necessary. He presented an appeal to the Christian women to go as missionaries to their sex. This resulted in the formation of a Woman's Missionary Society. It aimed at the education of the women of China and the East. Other societies were soon formed—as in Scotland in 1837. The Reformed have therefore the honor of suggesting the organization of the first of the Woman's Missionary Societies, which have done so much for the cause of missions.

He then sailed for America, and on account of his health spent the next winter in the South. But everywhere he spoke on missions. Much of his time was taken up in visiting colleges and theological seminaries. On his return from the South, he visited the churches of the Dutch Reformed denomination, producing a deep impression for missions. He also endeavored to organize the first Woman's Missionary Society in the United States, at the house of Mrs. Bethune, the mother of Rev. Dr. Bethune. Rev. Dr. Anderson, the secretary of the American Board, was present, but wished them to defer their organization. Mrs. Bethune answered him: "What! Are the American Board afraid that the ladies will get ahead of them?" Owing to Dr. Anderson's wish, there was a division among those present. Some were in favor of going on; others, out of respect for Dr. Anderson, were anxious to wait. Then Dr. Abeel, with tears rolling down his face, appealed to them to organize, saying: "What is to become of the souls of those who are ignorant of the offers of mercy and of the Bible?" Although no Woman's Society was organized then, yet his effort brought forth fruit later in the organization of the Union Missionary Society at New York in 1861, under Mrs. Doremus.

But he was again laid aside by sickness. He attempted to sail for China in October, 1836, but was prevented by a sudden attack of sickness. He was then sent to the West Indies to recuperate. While at St. Thomas, the physician discovered that he was suffering from an organic disease of the heart—an enlargement which interfered with the action of the lungs and might prove fatal at any moment. But being resigned either to live or die, he permitted nothing to interfere with his favorite work, and went on in his labors for the Lord. Just then, when his chances of returning to China seemed destroyed by ill health, he met the celebrated Dr. Griffin. After they had conversed together about the spiritual needs of Eastern Asia, Dr. Griffin prophetically said: "My son, your work is not yet done in China —the Lord has yet much for you to accomplish in that place for His glory." Finally, after spending his time as his health would permit in speaking in churches, colleges and seminaries about missions, he was able to sail, October 17, 1838.

He arrived at Canton on February 2, 1839, anxious to work for the Master. But again Providence hindered him, for the opium war broke out between England and China. He was therefore compelled to leave Canton for Macao, and then ordered to visit the different Dutch Reformed missions in Borneo. This war, in the providence of God, was the means of opening up China to missions. The Chinese wall of separation fell down like the walls of Jericho, and the set time to favor Sinim (China) had come. The prospect of having access to four hundred millions of souls was very exhilarating to him. He returned to China and landed at Amoy in 1842, ready to begin permanent mission work among the Chinese. He settled at the island of Kolongsou, about half a mile from Amoy, where he could live under British protection. And now began his real work among the Chinese. For twelve years he had been, like the Apostle Paul in Adria, driven up and down on the coast of China, without being able to find entrance. Now, however, he began laying the foundations of the successful Reformed mission at Amoy.

He was surprised at the beginning of his work to receive social visits from high Chinese officials. Evidently China was opening up to the Gospel. His audiences also increased. After having lived in these regions for so many years, fettered and tongue-tied, such liberty and receptivity on the part of the Chinese was delightful. In 1843 he attempted a tour inland, but found it very dangerous, as the inland Chinese were still bitter against foreigners. Still he scattered religious books and held personal conversation with many of the natives. In

June, 1844, he was very glad to welcome his fellow missionaries and successors, Doty and Pohlman. Nor did they come too soon, for two months later Dr. Abeel was compelled to leave his post on account of ill health.

He sailed for Hong Kong, and also visited the island of Quemoy, near Amoy. Here he greatly desired to settle, because of its delightful climate, but alas, he was not permitted to stay. He tried to preach in Chinese, but on account of his weakness and the irritation of his lungs, he was compelled to stop. His last sermon was on the text: "Come unto me, all ye that labor and are heavy laden, and I will give you rest," a very fitting topic with which such a sick man as he was should close his mission to the heathen. Worn out in body, he was compelled to return to America, April 3, 1845. To avoid the next cold winter, he went to Georgia, and then returned for the summer. Finally, on September 4, 1846, he fell asleep in Jesus at Albany, New York. Twelve days before he died he wrote: "Wonderfully preserved! With the kind and degree of disease which generally has a speedy issue, I live on. All things are mine. God sustains me through wearisome days and tedious, painful nights. When I embarked for home, the latter part of the fifth chapter of Hebrews was blessed to the production of the assurance of hope. I have not lost it. Death has no sting. Oh, may the Conqueror continue with me till the close and then!"

His life was an illustration, like Henry Martyn's, of how weakness of body can yet be used for great labors for God. No Foreign Mission Board today would think of sending out any one as sickly as Dr. Abeel, yet what a wonderful work he did. He was a man of no peculiar gifts of genius, but of great solidity and strength of character. His was rather the genius of spirituality, which elevated and made brilliant his powers. Rev. Dr. Anderson says of him: "Our brother was not a Paul, nor was he a Peter; he more resembled the beloved John. He was fitted to conciliate, to win. He was a good pioneer in a mission. It was a good thing for the Amoy mission that he was the one who commenced it. And to this, among other favoring Providences, we owe much of the peculiarly tolerant spirit among the leading Chinese of that place."

God has greatly blessed the mission which he was permitted to found. The Amoy mission, after more than fifty years of work, had 1,008 communicants.

In connection with the English Presbyterian mission there, it is doing a valuable work. That mission field will ever remain a living monument to perpetuate the memory of Abeel more grandly than does St. Paul's cathedral at London perpetuate the memory of Sir Christopher Wren. "Behold, these shall come from far, and lo, these from the north and from the west and these from the land of Sinim." Isa. 49:12.

Chapter V.
JOHN VAN NEST TALMAGE.

He belonged to the famous Talmage family, Rev. T. DeWitt Talmage, D.D., being a brother. He was born at Bound Brook, New Jersey, August 18, 1819. The home of his boyhood was a deeply religious one as is shown by the fact that four brothers from it entered the ministry. He graduated at Rutgers College in 1842, and from the Theological Seminary at New Brunswick in 1845. Missions early claimed his attention as a boy. Unknown to him his mother had devoted him to the work of missions. It was, however, an address by Rev. Mr. Doty, one of the missionaries of the Dutch Reformed Church, at Amoy, China, that finally led him to a decision. When he told his mother of his decision, "Oh, John," she exclaimed, "maternal love has its desire. I prayed God for this, and He has answered. How can I object?"

At seminary he showed such proficiency in the Greek and Hebrew that his name was later mentioned for that chair, but it was felt that he could not be spared from China. He was ordained at Millstone, New Jersey, August 26, 1846. The charge to him was given by Rev. Mr. Doty, the missionary. In the audience was a boy of eleven years of age who was so impressed by that service, that he later became a missionary to China, Rev. S. L. Baldwin, D.D., later Secretary of the Methodist Episcopal Missionary Society of the United States. As the Dutch Foreign Mission Board was not able to send him immediately because of lack of funds he temporarily became assistant to the Rev. Dr. Brodhead, of the Dutch Reformed church of Brooklyn, and might have become his successor had he desired, but his heart was set on China. When the Board was ready to send him they found him ready and waiting to go.

He sailed from New York April 15, 1847, and on August 19 he arrived at Amoy. He aimed to spend the first few years in learning the Chinese, but an unexpected event led to his return to America. Rev. Mr. Pohlman had been shipwrecked off the coast of China, an event which so unsettled the mind of his sister that it was deemed best to send her home, and Mr. Talmage was appointed to accompany her. He arrived at New York August 23, 1849. He then made an extensive tour through the churches of his denomination and re-embarked for China on March 16, 1850, arriving at Amoy July 16.

He was then placed in charge of a new enterprise in the northern part of Amoy, known as "At the Bamboos," where his chapel was opened December 23, 1850. There he preached, prayed and worked for nearly twenty years. By the following April he had thirteen converts. He thus tells the story of one of his early converts. The man gained a mere living by the profits of a small shop in which he sold paper candles to be used in their idolatrous worship. As he came under the influence of Christianity he found that his business was opposed to its doctrines. He had a hard struggle, but Christ conquered. He gave up the only prospect of making a livelihood, with no prospect before him and his family of anything but starvation.

A mason named Khi was led to become a Christian and then refused to work on Sunday. His employer told him he would discharge him if he did not work. But he still refused and was therefore discharged. After trying for some time to get work and failing, Dr. Talmage recommended him to a mason who was doing some work at the mission, and the latter gave him work. But his companions did not like his religion and soon had him discharged. As Dr. Talmage had an empty room on the first floor of his house, he let Khi stay there. Khi put together some empty boxes and laid some straw and a straw mat on them for his bed. He now tried to make a living by carrying potatoes about the street for sale, his profits being two to four cents a day. But in all his poverty he made no complaints. Winter came but he had no means to buy clothing or better food. Dr. Talmage said: "His room was right under my study. Almost every night I would hear his voice engaged in prayer before retiring to his straw. Sometimes he would pray a long, long time. The first thing in the morning I would hear would be his voice in prayer. I knew he was destitute, but did not dare aid him lest it might lead others to become Christians from unworthy motives." The poor man never complained. One day his voice was heard in prayer earlier than usual and soon after word came up to Dr. Talmage that Khi was sick. He went down and found him in the greatest destitution. He gave him medicine and good food and had his room made warm. The next day the missionary called him to his study to give him a little money with which to buy food and clothing, but had the greatest difficulty in making him take it. He had to call one of the natives to intercede with Khi to take the money, for the latter said that his sufferings were only for a short time, that they were much less than he deserved and were sent to teach him not to love the world.

Dr. Talmage early began literary work. Five years after his arrival he issued a primer which was followed by a translation of Pilgrim's Progress and parts of the New Testament. His most important literary work was in aiding to get the colloquial Chinese printed in the letters of our alphabet instead of in the difficult characters of the Chinese. His crowning work was his Amoy Colloquial Dictionary which brought light and knowledge to thousands who never could have gained it by reading with the harder Chinese characters.

In 1853 he passed through the "Little Knife" rebellion of China, which was led by the "Heaven and Earth Society," and which aimed to overthrow the Tartar dynasty from the throne of China. Amoy was attacked in May, 1853, and the rebels gained control of the city. He and his members held a quiet prayer meeting that Sunday, as they knew not what dangers were abroad. An evangelist in a neighboring town was beheaded. When the rebels gained control of the town the missionaries were fearful, as they did not know how they would feel toward foreigners. But as time wore on, they became somewhat used to the war scenes, and he humorously describes the results of a battle between the Chinese fleet and the rebels thus: "Killed none, wounded none, prisoners none." But it became more serious by and by, for his house was struck by a cannon ball. The shot struck a pillar and, if it had gone either side of it, it would have come into a room where many Chinese were gathered. When the army of the Chinese government again gained possession there was much shooting, but the foreigners were not hurt.

But the work of the Lord went on in spite of war. When he went to Amoy in 1847, the entire church membership of the mission was three. In 1850 it was five, by the end of 1851 it was nineteen. In 1854-1855 there was a great revival. His congregation rejoiced at receiving twenty-eight in 1854. He tells an interesting story of one of them, a widow who lived about fifteen miles from Amoy. Once "when she came to town she determined to enter the missionary's house to see how foreigners lived. As she entered she was met by the person who had charge of the chapel. He asked her business. She replied she had only come for amusement. He replied, 'This is no place of amusement but to hear the doctrine.' 'Well,' she said, 'then I will hear the doctrine.' He explained to her some of the truths of Christianity. He told her that after breakfast I would be in the chapel for worship. She went to a neighbor to get her breakfast. But the new doctrine of which she had heard took such a hold on her mind that she desired no breakfast for herself. As she listened to the missionary with wonder, she said: 'This doctrine cannot be of man. It must be the great power of God.' From that time she was almost always present, coming from her home almost every week to hear the gospel. She brought her two sons with her, desiring that they should become Christians, and also brought some of her neighbors. She met with much persecution but bore it all patiently. After her baptism she rented a room at Amoy. When the missionary asked her how she expected to maintain herself at Amoy, she replied: 'If she could not get as good food as others she would eat coarser bread.'" How great is the self-denial of the heathen convert! Among the inquirers were two lads who were severely beaten by their parents for their determination to follow Christ.

Dr. Talmage says: "The elder of them was scourged yesterday. This morning he is again tied up in a very painful manner and beaten by his father. He carried the marks on his arms which were visible, and had others on his body. We trust they are the marks of the Lord Jesus."

When the negotiations for the union of denominations on the mission field were begun with the Presbyterian church of England, he heartily favored the union. When, in 1863, the General Synod of the Dutch Reformed Church refused to allow their mission to join with these English Presbyterians in China, Dr. Talmage stood his ground on the floor of the General Synod. Though defeated that year, yet the next year his arguments prevailed and the General Synod reconsidered its action and ordered the union of those two denominations which has been so richly blessed of God. The years 1870-1871 were years of trial to him on account of the anti-missionary agitation. In Canton vile stories were concocted, i. e., that the foreigners distributed poisonous pills, etc. The ferment soon reached Amoy. Inflammatory placards were posted up even with the support of the Chinese officials. Foreigners were called "little demons," and were charged with poisoning the wells. Native Christians had to suffer much persecution. Fortunately the war cloud blew over and the opposition ceased.

In 1889 Dr. Talmage returned to America expecting to go back again to China. But God decreed it otherwise. Forty-two years of active service had so overworked him that he died at the home of his boyhood, Bound Brook, N. J., August 19, 1892, aged 73 years. Says Rev. Dr. E. T. Corwin: "He stood in the front rank of missionaries. He spoke the Chinese language like themselves, beautifully and idiomatically. For ability, for fidelity, for usefulness he had few equals." This Amoy mission of the Dutch Reformed Church reported in 1901, 1,392 communicants.

CHAPTER VI.

WILLIAM E. HOY AND THE NEW MISSION OF THE REFORMED CHURCH IN THE UNITED STATES.

In 1899 the General Synod of the Reformed Church in the United States decided to open a new mission in China. The Board, therefore, ordered Rev. W. E. Hoy, one of its missionaries to Japan, to go to China as the Japanese climate did not at all agree with his health. He had previously visited China, seeking relief, and was, therefore, familiar with it. His letters and appeals to the home church, made after the Japan-Chinese war, had been the main instrument in leading the church to take up this new mission, and it was, therefore, very fitting that he should be appointed to it. He at once went to China and after canvassing the situation, selected the newly opened province of Hunan, in Central China, as the location of the mission. This province had, a few years before, most bitterly opposed Christianity, all sorts of scandalous circulars and tales having been circulated about it. But since that time even the ringleader in that movement had become an inquirer into Christianity. So great a change had come over it that even in the Boxer rebellion the province was little affected against foreigners.

Mr. Hoy had been a pioneer already in the mission in Japan. He had been one of the very first to go to Sendai to open the new mission there. With Rev. Mr. Oshikawa he had been instrumental in opening a boys' school there which afterward grew into a College and Theological Seminary. When he was about starting it, a poor widow came to him, bringing twelve pieces of silver which she had collected to defray her funeral expenses and offered it toward the founding of a school to educate evangelists. Thus encouraged, he started with six young men, supporting them the first years himself. A pioneer in Japan, he was fitted to be a pioneer in Central China, too. He chose Yochou, near Hankow, in Central China, as the seat of the new mission. In 1902 the Board purchased the mission property of the London Missionary Society at that place, which at once gave the mission a starting point and center. The mission has since been strengthened by the sending out of the first medical missionary, Dr. Albert Beam and his wife, who is also a physician, together with Rev. W. A. Reimert and Miss Emma Ziemer, who goes as a teacher. Already the nucleus of a school has been formed. A hospital and dispensary will be opened and the work will spread in influence and increase in its results and will doubtless be a factor in the regeneration of the land of Sinim (China).

REV. DR. VERBECK IN 1897.

C.—Japan.

Chapter VII.

GUIDO F. VERBECK.

One of the greatest of modern missionaries of the nineteenth century was Rev. Dr. Verbeck. Few men have been accorded such great opportunities for political as well as religious influence. "Verbeck of Japan the greatest under God of the makers of the new nation that is coming, and even now is," is the description by his biographer about his work in Japan. He stood as one of the sponsors at the founding of the new Japan, politically. He was also the one who baptized the first Protestant convert in Japan. He was a many-sided man, first an engineer, then a preacher, then a teacher and translator.

He was born at Zeist in Holland, January 23, 1830, his father having been a German Moravian pastor there. He there joined the Moravian church and attended their school. From the Moravians he received some of his missionary inspiration and a visit to Zeist by Gutzlaff, the great Chinese missionary, he never forgot. At this Moravian school he became master of four languages: Dutch, German, English and French, and thus began his remarkable linguistic preparation for his great future.

As he was born in the year that railways were introduced into Holland, his parents thought he must become an engineer. He, therefore, went to the Polytechnic school at Utrecht. Through the invitation of his brother-in-law, Rev. Mr. Van Deurs, he was led to come to this new world in 1852, and located at Green Bay, Wisconsin, where he had charge of a foundry. He tried to revolutionize himself into an Americanized Dutchman, for he says: "I am determined to become a good Yankee." From Green Bay he was led to take a position at Helena, Arkansas, as draftsman and engineer. It was while here that he was prostrated by a severe illness which led him to more serious reflection, and he covenanted with God that if He would spare his life he would consecrate his life to Him as a missionary. He returned to Green Bay in 1854. In the autumn of 1855 his brother-in-law, Rev. Mr. Van Deurs, influenced him to go to the Theological Seminary at Auburn, New York. There he revealed fine abilities as a student and as a singer, preaching also to a German congregation in Auburn.

Meanwhile great changes were taking place on the other side of the globe preparing for his future work. Ray Palmer said more than fifty years ago:

"I fancy I am coming back to the world five hundred years from now and I shall see Japan opened to the Gospel." He did not need to wait twenty-five years. Commodore Perry had conquered Japan without firing a gun, and that hitherto hermit land was thrown open to the gospel. The Dutch Reformed Board had decided to locate a mission there and was looking around for an Americanized Dutchman to go there as missionary. It was believed that, as the only Protestant nation with whom Japan had had any business relations hitherto was Holland, a Dutchman would probably have peculiar influence, especially as that language had hitherto been Japan's only medium of intercourse with the west. So he was appointed by the Board February 16, 1859. He was ordained by the Presbytery of Cayuga March 22, and received by the Reformed Classis of Cayuga the next day. Before going to Japan he deemed it wise to take out papers of American citizenship but found he was unable to comply with the laws on the subject. He had no claim to citizenship in Holland as his father had been a German and not a Dutchman. He could not become an American citizen. He therefore lived "a man without a country," although a resident of three lands, Holland, the

United States and Japan. But he did not need it. God protected him; his citizenship was on high. He sailed from New York May 7, 1859, and reached Nagasaki, Japan, on November 7, 1859, after a voyage of about six months.

His life in Japan can be divided into three periods of about ten years each; the first as a missionary at Nagasaki, the second as an educator at Tokio, the third as a translator and evangelist. He first began to learn the language which he, with his fine linguistic powers, so mastered that the Japanese said he was the only foreigner who could speak their language without his foreign nationality being known, so correct was his pronunciation and idiom. His early life at Nagasaki was in the time of danger. When he arrived there, Japan was still unsettled about its reception of foreigners and foreign ideas. Some of the foreigners were assassinated by the reactionaries. But quietly through all the changes Verbeck went on with his work. When he arrived at Japan the edict-boards, threatening death to any one who was a Christian, were still seen along the roads.

He found he could do little more than study the language and make friends with the people. He however had a class of two young men whom he instructed in the Bible as well as in English. These young men were twice promoted and to show their gratitude to Dr. Verbeck they presented him with two black sucking pigs, which, humorously says Griffis, his biographer, "showed that their idea of foreigners was that they were fond of pork." The governor of Nagasaki found the two Japanese students of Verbeck so useful that while Verbeck left the country, 1863-4, because of the political upheavals there, he conceived the idea of a training school for interpreters and asked Dr. Verbeck to act as principal in 1866. (From that time till 1878 he was self-supporting because in government employ.) His school soon had over one hundred pupils. It brought him into contact with the brightest minds of the young men of Japan. Into this school came prominent young men, as the two sons of the prime minister Iwakura and others, who were destined to occupy high office in the Japan that was to come. By June 10, 1866, he had the joy of seeing two of his pupils, the nephews of Yokoi Heishiro, start for America, the first of a procession of five hundred or more who were aided by the Dutch Reformed Church of America.

He then had the honor of baptizing the first Japanese Christian. Murata, the lord of Wakasa and commander of the army of his province, had been guarding the harbor of Nagasaki against foreigners in 1855. There he came into contact with the few Dutchmen who had been allowed to trade with Japan. One of them gave him a picture of the seige of Sebastopol in the Crimean War, which greatly impressed him. He sought to learn the secret of the power of Christian nations. He frequently went out at night in a boat to inspect his guard. On one of these occasions he saw floating on the water a little book, different in language, type and binding from anything he had yet seen. He became interested in it, after finding an interpreter who could read it, for it was a Dutch Bible. It told him about the Creator of the universe and about Jesus. The more he heard, the more he wanted to hear. He sent one of his men to Nagasaki ostensibly to study medicine, but really to find out from the Dutch more about this book. When he heard there was a Chinese translation of it, he secretly sent to China and got it. His home was at Saga where he secretly began the study of the New Testament.

God was arranging to bring Murata and Verbeck

together. One of the two young men who first began to study English with Verbeck was Ayabe, Murata's younger brother. Ayabe went to Nagasaki in 1862 in order to gain an understanding of the Bible. There he met Dr. Verbeck who answered his questions about the meanings of the various passages of Scripture. Afterward he sent his relative Montono to Nagasaki to study English and the Bible. Dr. Verbeck taught Wakasa through this channel, Montono serving faithfully as a messenger between them carrying questions and answers back and forth for nearly three years.

Finally, on May 14, 1866, Murata with Ayabe and Motono visited Verbeck. The conversation lasted for hours. Murata said: "Sir, I cannot tell you my feelings when I first read the account of Jesus' character. I had never heard of such a person. I was filled with admiration, overwhelmed with emotion and taken captive by His nature and life." Then Murata asked for baptism for himself and his younger brother. Verbeck warned them that there was no magic in baptism to save them and also warned them of the danger in which they would place themselves in Japan if they became Christians. But they were willing to suffer all if necessary. So on the next Sunday (May 20, 1866) the three men, Murata, Ayabe and Motono, were baptized in Dr. Verbeck's parlor at Nagasaki, and they there joyfully joined together in celebrating the Lord's Supper. The matter was kept somewhat quiet. Murata reported it, but the prince seeing his firmness left them alone. The Japanese government ordered Murata's punishment, but all that was done was to burn some of his books. He lived a Christian life and died in 1874.

The revolution of 1868 was essentially a students' revolution, and when it was successful the young men in Tokio felt the need of wise counsel. Instinctively they turned to their old teacher, Verbeck, of Nagasaki. They invited him to Tokio to lay the foundations of the Imperial University. Although these men were not Christians neither did they desire a Christian government, yet they felt that in Verbeck they had a man upon whose judgment they could rely, and on whose integrity they could rest. "Nowhere," says Bliss, "in the annals of history has there a grander opportunity come to any man, and nowhere has the opportunity been more nobly used."

He went to Tokio in 1870, and through his influence two very important political movements were begun. He organized the Imperial University, appointing teachers and attending to its many details. He was authorized by the government to call teachers from America to aid in the new education of Japan. By 1873 the school had five hundred students, and eighteen teachers of four nationalities.

The other important movement was his proposition of an embassy from Japan to the United States to study its institutions. This embassy came here in 1872. The whole arrangement of it—its plan, personnel, etc.—was entrusted to him. He was surprised to find that half of the embassy had been pupils of his. His statesmanship was so highly appreciated that Iwakura, the prime minister, frequently consulted him on the gravest affairs of the State. Griffis, his biographer who taught in Japan in 1870, says: "I saw a prime minister of the empire, heads of departments and officers of various ranks come to him for information and advice. Today it might be a plan of national education, tomorrow the dispatch of an envoy to Europe, the choice of a language best suited to medical science, how to act about neutrality between France and Germany, how to learn the truth about some foreign diplomat or concerning the persecutions of Christians or some serious measure of home policy." All this showed the great confidence of the government in his judgment and wisdom.

In 1874 a change began to come over the Japanese. Opposition to Christianity began to lift its head. One of its first signs was an attempt to abolish Sunday as a day of rest. But Verbeck refused to submit. With the other English-speaking teachers, both American and British, he protested against it as a breach of the contract made with them by the Japanese government. He then sent a note to Mr. Iwakura who speedily settled the matter to his satisfaction. In 1873 he was transferred to the service of the senate. Here his main duty was translator of legal books and documents. He aided them in the formation of a national constitution of 1889 and the treaties of 1898 by which Japan took her place among the civilized nations of the world. He thus became not only the founder of the Imperial University, but a maker of the great Japan of the future. In 1877, when he resigned from his position, the emperor, to show his appreciation of his work, bestowed on him, although a foreigner, the third class order of the Rising Sun. Its insignia was a central circle containing a fine large ruby. The circle is surrounded by pointed rays in gold, filled in with white enamel, the colors being those of Japan, and the symbol that of the sun shining in its strength. Above the symbol is the three-leaved blossom of the kiri tree (the Paulonia Imperialis), the three flowers surmounting the leaves all in gold, the leaves being in green and the flowers in purple enamel. The Paulonia flower is the Emperor's family crest. Of it Verbeck wrote: "This is the first piece of jewelry I ever owned and also indirectly a tribute to the cause of missions." This decoration was not only an honor but was also of value to him at times. Thus on one occasion when, owing to a fire, he could not get through the streets of Tokio to an important engagement, he simply showed this decoration on the lapel of his coat to a policeman and immediately the way was made for him. While thus attending to State and school engagements he was also active in the Reformed church at the capital, the Kojimachi church.

The last period of his life (1877-98) was one of evangelism and translation. He went everywhere through the empire preaching with wonderful power. He had been teaching in the Nobles School, but now gave himself especially to spiritual work. Great crowds attended his preaching tours.

In 1889 he returned to America visiting his birthplace, Zeist, in Holland, on the way. He also awakened great missionary interest in Holland by his addresses. In 1891 he returned to Japan where he was busy lecturing in the Nobles School and in the theological seminary and in preaching. He was also busy in translating the Bible which he had begun in 1881, and whose completion he lived to see. The translation was so good that the Psalms were compared in beauty and majesty to the famous Japanese mountain Fujiyama. One of his last works was the preparation of an address to be presented to the Emperor of Japan on the occasion of the presentation of the Japanese Bible to him. His great activity continued until 1897, when his physician forbade his evangelistic tours. He died suddenly on March 10, 1898, while sitting in his study-chair just after he had taken his noon meal.

Some of the highest officers and noblemen of the empire attended his funeral, the Emperor sending $250 to pay the expenses and ordered two companies of soldiers to attend the body to the grave, the burial lot being deeded by the city government. Thus, although he was a citizen of no country, Japan tried to show its appreciation of his great services to her in education, statesmanship and religion. So lived and so died the man who fashioned the young men who made Japan. Probably no missionary in the nineteenth century, except Livingston, exerted so far-reaching and so lasting a political influence for Christianity. In moulding the Sunrise Kingdom, he moulded the Orient of the twentieth century. The two greatest missionaries of the nineteenth century, in their political influence as well as religious, have been David Livingston, who opened up Africa, and Guido F. Verbeck, who laid the foundations of Japan. The first was the greatest missionary to the continent of Africa, the other the greatest missionary to the continent of Asia. The first was laid away in Westminster Abbey amid all the honors of England, the last buried at Tokio amid all the honors of Japan.

CHAPTER VIII.

THE MISSION OF THE REFORMED CHURCH IN THE UNITED STATES.

This Church having supported Rev. Benjamin Schneider, D.D., in Turkey for twenty-five years, and after that Rev. Oscar Lohr in India for a number of years, finally determined in 1878 at its General Synod, to have a mission of its own. Its Board chose Japan as its field, and on September 30, 1878, it appointed its first missionary thither, Rev. Ambrose D. Gring. He sailed May, 1879, arriving at Yokohama, Japan, June 1, 1879, thus making June 1, 1904, the quarter-century anniversary of the establishment of the Japan mission. The Board on April 26, 1880, chose Tokio, the capital of Japan, as its centre, and to it the missionary removed in June, 1880. Mr. Gring was reinforced by Rev. J. B. Moore on October 1, 1883, and the first congregation was organized May 11, 1884, at Nihon Bashi, Tokio, by these two missionaries. Mr. Gring returned to this country in 1887 and resigned from the service of the Board in 1889. Mr. Moore meanwhile continued the work with gratifying success as the Japanese at that time were very cordial toward foreigners, especially for the sake of learning English. The influence of the mission began to show itself in many ways even among the upper classes through the labors of Mr. Moore and his wife. Mrs. Moore, in the spring of 1886, had formed a class of ladies belonging rather to the upper class for the study of English and the reading of the Bible, the explanations being interpreted by an assistant. In this class was a Mrs. Nakajima, who soon gave proof that she cared more for the study of the Bible than merely for the study of English. She requested by and by that her husband might be allowed to accompany her. Mr. Moore had learned that both had been reading the Bible at home, so he felt no hesitation at inviting Mr. Nakajima to become a member of his Wednesday evening Bible class, conducted in English and interpreted by his personal teacher. Both became regular attendants of the Bible class and also of the Sunday afternoon services, held in the dining room of his house. On the 18th of July, 1886, these two, with four others, were baptized in the parlor of the missionary's house at Bancho, Tokio. Mr. Nakajima had already been a man of prominence in political affairs, having served as a member of the senate and governor of the province in which Yokohama is located. On the 25th of November, 1890, when Japan had become a constitutional monarchy, he was elected president of the lower House of Japan, having the highest number of votes and being one of three candidates submitted to the Emperor for appointment. The Emperor appointed him. He has since been Minister of Japan to Italy. His wife has been a poet and the authoress of several popular novels.

But Providence was preparing the mission for a new centre of operations. Mr. Moore was called from the service of the mission to become a teacher at Yamagata in northern Japan. He accepted the position on condition that he would be allowed to speak of Christ, although a government teacher. As a result a Y. M. C. A. sprang up there, and a small congregation which is now under the care of Rev. H. Miller. He afterward became a teacher in the government school at Sendai.

Meanwhile the Lord was preparing Sendai, in northern Japan, to become the centre of our operations. Christian preaching had been started at Niigata by a medical missionary, Dr. Palm, and he sent to Tokio for some one to act as pastor. The pastor of the Dutch Reformed Church at Tokio made the appeal for a missionary known to his congregation. Now there was in his congregation an elder named Masayoshi Oshikawa. He was born December 16, 1850. When nineteen years of age he was selected, with several other young men, by their feudal lord to be sent to the Imperial English College at Tokio so as to be fitted for prominent positions in the government service. In order to learn English, although bitterly opposed to Christianity, he yet became a pupil of one of the Dutch Reformed missionaries, Rev. James Ballagh, D.D. But the text-book used in the teaching of English was the Bible. And the more he read it in English the more he read it into his own heart. One day after he had been studying it for nine months, Mr. Ballagh held a prayer meeting, and at its close he said: "If any one of you desires to be a Christian, let him place a card with his name on my table." To his surprise he found the next morning the names of nine students, one of them Oshikawa's.

He had hardly confessed Christ than he was called to his home five hundred miles away. There he suffered severe persecutions for having become a Christian, his father threatening to take his life if he did not return to heathenism. He afterwards learned that it was only through the interposition of his mother that his life was spared, although she had often appealed to him most tenderly for her sake to return to heathenism. But he stood firm. None of these things moved him, neither tears nor threats. He was finally bidden to leave home and went to Tokio, where he arrived penniless. He then studied theology for four years under Rev. S. R. Brown, D.D., of the Dutch Reformed Church, the son of the authoress of that beautiful hymn "I love to steal awhile away." While doing this he became an elder in the Dutch Reformed church. Then came the call of Dr. **Palm**.

It was on a Week of Prayer at the beginning of the year that this call came from Dr. Palm for a missionary to live among them. There was no money to send any one, nor did any one seem ready to go. But the members of the church took the matter to God in prayer. Finally Oshikawa rose at the end of the meeting and said: "I must and will go." His friends recounted to him the difficulties, but he simply replied: "I must and will go." So he was, after prayer, consecrated to the work. As he was very poor, Dr. Brown gave him three of his own suits, fur gloves and boots. Unfortunately the coats were much too large and the boots too small, but fit or no fit, he would go. It was a long journey over the mountains to Niigata from whence the call came. He lost his way, was weary and hungry and was about to lie down in the snow and die. But just then there rang out in the air the sound of an ax. He made his way a little farther on and found eleven woodcutters who took him to their cave and gave him a cupful of cold and dirty rice. He fell asleep. On waking the first words he heard were "Jesu Kirisuto," the Japanese for "Jesus Christ." These men were reading a copy of the New Testament that they had received from a missionary the previous summer. They could not understand what they read. They had, however, formed a temperance society, taking the Ten Commandments as their constitution. Finding he was a Christian they asked him to stay a week. He stayed three days, preaching and teaching. The next summer they were all baptized, and some of them became preachers of the gospel.

He then went on his way and soon arrived at the Niigata. But this town was a stronghold of the Buddhist religion, and great was the opposition.

He was stoned, beaten, spat upon. Women poured dish water and boiling water on him as he passed through the streets. The mob determined to put him to death.

The mayor of the city resembled him in appearance. One morning as that official was on his way to his office, some members of the mob saw him in the distance and raised the cry: "Here comes that Jesus-man. Come, let's kill him." A large crowd gathered and gave chase. The mayor ran into the police sentry box on the corner of two streets and locked the door after him. The mob rushed up, tore off the roof, and lifted the man out bodily and violently put him to death. Oshikawa was very much affected by this. He said: "Two persons have died for me, Jesus of Nazareth, the Son of the living God has died for me. And now the faithful mayor of this city has died in my stead." Still God protected his life as he preached, and he reported fourteen converts.

But a fire broke out in Niigata burning 9,000 houses, and there was no place where they could hold service. So Dr. Palm and Mr. Oshikawa left and went to Sendai where the people seemed to be more friendly and because it was a more important place than Niigata. His audiences soon became large and interesting. In 1887 they purchased an old Buddhist temple as a place of worship which seated five hundred. Two years previously (1885) Mr. Oshikawa and his congregation made application to be received into the United Church of Japan which is composed of the Presbyterian and Reformed churches in that land. He, however, stipulated two conditions: 1. The establishing of a Boys' and Girls' School. 2. The supply of money for evangelistic purposes. Just about this time the mission of our church was received into the United Church of Japan. And in its division of Japan among the different denominations composing that church, our church was given northern Japan. This new church at Sendai therefore came into our district and we received without any effort or expense to ourselves the largest church north of Tokio into our mission, a church of three congregations and two hundred members.

In 1886 W. E. Hoy, the third missionary sent by our church, located at Sendai. He, with Mr. Oshikawa, started the Boys' School which has since grown into a College and Theological Seminary, of which the president at present is Rev. D. B. Schneder, D.D. These have done a most excellent work in training up especially ministers and evangelists for our mission.

A very interesting story of this Boys' School is that of one of its students, Dengoro Takahashi. He was born June 15, 1871. He had gone to Tokio and taken an examination in the Military School, for he was zealous for the military glory of his country, but failed. He bitterly hated Christianity. But as he could not study at Tokio, he left and finally was led to go to Sendai where, in his thirst for an education, he entered the Industrial School of our mission. He also began searching the truths of Christianity and was finally baptized. His next step was to become a student for the ministry in the Theological School. He became very active in religious work at Sendai.

It happened that the Japanese were at that time very anxious to enlarge their borders and colonize. No place seemed open to them but the islands of the Pacific. Lieutenant Gunji, therefore, organized a colonization society to colonize the Kurile islands, and on his way thither, in the fall of 1893, he called to see Mr. Oshikawa. The latter urged the lieutenant to take some one along to look after the religious interests of the colonists. The lieutenant finally yielded and said, "Have you any students who would be willing to go?" "Yes, we have many," replied Oshikawa, and Takahashi, who was standing by, said: "Here am I. I will go." Although he expected to face death in this expedition, he feared nothing. At the farewell meeting in the Sendai church he said he "hoped to make his bones the pillars of a church and his flesh its walls." His going caused a sensation in Japan, for by it the Christians were doing more than the native religions of Japan by sending a missionary to look after the religious welfare of the colonists.

When they arrived in the Kurile islands he, with eight others, were left on one of them. When one of the Japanese men-of-war went there later, they found him with the others dead, suffocated probably by the charcoal fumes of their fire, about the 11th of December, 1893. The news of it came to Japan when the Synod of the United Church of Japan was holding its session, and at once there was weeping and great sorrow. But he "being dead yet speaketh," like Abel. The sacrifice of his young life in missionary work for Christ proved an inspiration to the native church, and gave to the heathen a wonderful example of Christian bravery and testimony.

A Girls' School was also started by Miss Lizzie R. Poorbaugh and Miss Mary B. Ault in 1886. The ground for it was purchased by Rev. J. I. Swander, D.D., and wife, of Tiffin, Ohio, and a school building built upon it. The school flourished and outgrew its quarters until in the spring of 1902 it was burned down. Both these institutions have been greatly blessed, and have exerted a blessed influence in northern Japan.

The following is a list of the missionaries not yet mentioned, but who have been in connection with the mission: Rev. S. S. Snyder, Rev. C. Noss, Paul L. Gerhard, Rev. H. H. Cook and Rev. J. M. Stick; and as teachers in the Girls' School, Miss Emma F. Poorbaugh, Lena Zurfluh, Mary C. Hallowell, L. M. Rohrbaugh, Sadie L. Weidner, Lucy M. Powell and Catharine B. Peiffer.

The last report of the mission for 1902 showed it had 2,142 communicants, of whom 335 were added in 1901. There are 56 stations and outstations, and three schools with 269 scholars.

REV. DR. BENJAMIN SCHNEIDER.

D.—Mohammedan Lands.

CHAPTER IX.

BENJAMIN C. SCHNEIDER.

This earnest minister was the pioneer missionary of the Reformed Church in the United States to the heathen. He was their missionary so long ago that we fear many in the Church have forgotten him. But he needs to be remembered as the forerunner of our Foreign Mission work in Japan. Dr. Schneider sowed the seed and interested the Church in the salvation of the heathen; and we in our day are reaping the results in a heathen land far distant from the one in which he labored. The younger generation who have come up since his labors should be instructed in them so that this honored missionary may receive the honor due to him.

Benjamin C. Schneider was born at New Haven, Montgomery county, Pennsylvania, January 18, 1807. He was the son of an elder in our Church in Montgomery county. His early studies were at Norristown Academy at which place he united with the Presbyterian Church. He attended Amherst College, graduating 1830, and graduated from Andover Theological Seminary in 1833. The same year he sailed for Turkey as a foreign missionary. At that time most of the denominations in America did their foreign mission work through the American Board of Foreign Missions. Our Church had as yet no Board of its own.

That Board gave our Church a representative in their Executive Committee by electing Rev. Prof. J. W. Nevin, D.D., of the Theological Seminary at Mercersburg, a member, and he served as a member of the American Board for twenty-five years, 1840-1865. Our Church was therefore united with that Board during that time, and contributed during these years nearly $28,000 for his support. And as Mr. Schneider was by birth a member of the Reformed Church, though educated in the Presbyterian, he returned to her and became a member of one of her Classes, the Maryland Classis, with which he remained connected till his death in 1877.

He thus became the representative of our Church, and his work in Turkey was looked upon as our work. When he arrived in Turkey, he settled at Broosa—famous for its Turkish silks. Here he studied the Turkish language and revealed his fine linguistic abilities. For he was able to speak in three languages besides his own—Turkish, German and Greek, as easily as English. After he had mastered the Turkish, he preached the first evangelical sermon there ever preached in that language. He became so proficient in it that the Turks often wondered at his marvelous flow of thought expressed in their peculiar idioms and phrases. We are sure that in his preaching at Broosa he offered them a robe more precious than all Oriental silks, the robe of Christ's righteousness.

But his main field of operations was at Aintab, whither he removed in 1849, and remained for about twenty years. There like the Apostle Paul, he was more abundant in labors. The work of the American Board there was among the Armenian Christians, whose service is very much like that of the Romish Church. They had been unaccustomed to hearing the gospel in their own language. The origin of this church at Aintab is quite interesting. First, some copies of the New Testament happened to be sold there. A few of the people who were able to read, bought them. By and by a company of Scripture-readers was formed, who asked for further instruction, and missionaries and colporteurs began to visit the town. There was great opposition at first, and in 1847, two years before Dr.

Schneider went there, Rev. T. C. Johnston was ordered to leave, and was stoned when he left. His meekness under such an insult, so impressed one of the young men who helped in the stoning, that he soon became a convert, and has been for many years a deacon in the church. Then cholera came with its awful ravages, and a skilful Protestant physician went there, Dr. Azariah Smith. He organized a church of eight members, in January, 1848. To this charge Dr. Schneider came in 1849. He had spent the previous summer there, and the following spring he brought his family there to remain permanently. He laid the foundations of two large and influential churches, which have since increased into a third. He greatly loved to preach the gospel, and the effect of his preaching was great. A native physician who was converted through his instrumentality, says: "The Holy Spirit seemed always to be present when Dr. Schneider was preaching. I still remember distinctly, sermons preached by him thirty years ago—not the text only, but the heads and the illustrations, and the fervent appeals which were irresistible." He would often walk the floor after preaching to those large audiences in Aintab, in an ecstasy of delight, saying: "I would rather preach the gospel to this people, than be a king on any throne." His works remain behind him. Three of the professors in the college at Aintab, are sons of his first converts. A wealthy merchant who has just erected a splendid Y. M. C. A. building, was his pupil, one of his first converts. We feel like giving part of a letter written to Mrs. Schneider, by one who knew and loved him at Aintab. It reads thus: "Our third congregation at Aintab has outgrown its accommodations, and a few days since I went with those who have the work in charge to see the larger rooms they propose to rent for a chapel. My heart was full, for these were the rooms occupied for so many years by Rev. Dr. Schneider and his goodly wife, whose grave is among the people she loved. We looked into the good man's study—into the sitting room and the bed rooms; discussed removing this and that wall, so as to accommodate three hundred people—my thoughts meanwhile dwelling on those early days, when these very walls witnessed the prayers and the tears of that devoted missionary and his wife, as they sowed the seed that has borne, so rich a harvest. Returning home, we found our weekly mail with the tidings that this servant of God had passed to his rest—his reward. The first emotion that swept over me, was of joyful congratulation for him, the second of deep and tearful gratitude that God gave me such a friend and father, when He called me to this blessed work many years ago. Battel Bey (a very wicked Turkish governor) told his physician that his friend, Schneider, was a wonderfully holy man—so holy, that if he would accept the prophet (Mohammed) he would be received to heaven without passing the judgment, and with no questions asked—that few, very few, are found who work with such simplicity and singleness of purpose, as he did. For this reason he had great influence over those men who were considered hard to approach, and that, also in regard to those subjects in which they are least approachable, as personal religion, and liberality of giving for the cause of Christ. When he was preaching in a temporary chapel, soon after his coming to Aintab, four young men, gay and irreligious, went to hear what this 'setter forth of strange doctrines' had to say. Not wishing to attract notice, they went up to the flat earthen roof, and sat down beside a large hole which had been opened for ventilation, where they could look down upon the preacher, and hear his words very distinctly, being themselves, as they thought, secure from observation. After the opening exercises, Dr. Schneider arose, adjusted his spectacles, gave the group on the roof one full look, and announced his text, John 15: 5 and 6. 'I am the vine, ye are the branches,' etc. You know the spirit that always seemed to be speaking through Dr. Schneider. Our attention was riveted, and ever and anon, the preacher would fix his eyes upon us, and ask some pointed question, so that we trembled and wept as we sat there, and afterwards went home together for a season of prayer for mercy, for we felt we were indeed only withered branches fit to be burned. All four of these young men soon became Christians, and continue steadfast. One is an evangelist, one, the narrator, is a deacon of the church, and a prominent physician. He is still able to report with minuteness, many of the sermons which he heard thirty years ago."

The recent kidnapping of Miss Stone in Bulgaria reminds us of a similar scene in the life of Dr. Schneider, in November, 1853. His wife graphically tells the story in a letter to one of her daughters in this country. She says:

"I was expecting your father home this afternoon, as he had important reasons for wishing to get home as rapidly as possible. Dinner was waiting till nearly night, yet he did not come, when a messenger arrived, bringing the news of their having fallen in with robbers. They had nearly reached the place where they were to spend the night, when three men who had been walking either before or behind for nearly two hours, and armed with swords, pistols, habergeons and clubs, rushed out from among the bushes, each one grasping a bridle of the three mules—that is of father, of the native brother, and of the guide. Mrs. Pratt, seeing the blows they inflicted and fearing they would be murdered, whipped up her horse and tried to flee. They struck poor father many times violently, pulled him off of his horse, threw him on the ground, took his money, his watch, his fez, and thought of taking his fur-garment and horse; but fearing they would be detected by the last named, left them. They threatened him several times with instant death. He received a blow upon his head, and a profusion of blood was the consequence. His arm also received a blow; his side a kick, which caused him much pain. At the time one villain stood over him with a drawn sword saying, 'I will kill you this instant.' Mrs. Pratt was brought back by one of them who ran after her. She supposed she was to be murdered, as she supposed the others had been, for the native brother was thrown, bound and blinded, upon the ground and father, too, was in the same condition, with a garment thrown over him. On Mrs. Pratt's arrival he moved one of his limbs, and because of this, as if intending to rise and deliver himself, one of the villains rushed upon him with a drawn sword threatening him with instant death if he spoke a word. Poor Mrs. Pratt, who had displayed such fortitude, seeing him about to inflict a deadly wound, raised both her hands towards heaven and cried, 'Oh dear, oh dear, he is a missionary,' as if such a fact would restrain him. She, too, was robbed of all the money she had with her, about $20. They escaped and came back tonight, in the most painful condition. I have dressed father's wounds, which, though not deadly, give him most excruciating pain. He speaks only of God's mercy."

Dr. Schneider adds that when the robber had raised his hand to kill him, that he thought his last hour had come, and expected every moment to feel the deadly weapon on some part of his body. Nothing but an Almighty arm restrained the ruffian. He says that they were kept in that condition about three quarters of an hour, when the robbers, having rifled everything in their baggage, as well as on themselves, fled. He said, that up to that time, that part of the road had not been considered dangerous, or they would have taken guards.

Turkey does not seem to have improved much in fifty years as far as safety is concerned. But such events impress upon us the great importance of prayer for our missionaries far away in heathen lands, that their lives and health may be spared.

In 1856, after his first wife died (who had been a Miss Eliza C. Abbott, of Framingham, Mass.), he returned to this country, and spent about two years here. Part of his time was spent in visiting the Reformed churches, and stirring them up to greater interest and zeal for the salvation of the heathen. Everywhere he carried the missionary spirit into the churches and the homes. One of the clearest boyish recollections of the writer was when Dr. Schneider visited the home of his father, and laid his hand on his head (he was about seven years of age) and asked him whether he would become a missionary, and he promised. Thus Dr. Schneider labored everywhere for missions, both at home and abroad. Before he returned to Turkey he married the sister of his first wife, Miss Susan M. Abbott (who survived his death and lived after it at Boston, Mass.). At Aintab, his work in the girls' school, was a powerful agency for good. One hundred and sixty girls have graduated there, and as teachers, Bible women and heads of families, exert a wide influence for Christianity. We can only properly measure the greatness of this work, when it is remembered that when he went to Aintab, there was only one woman who could read.

In 1868, he left Aintab, to live at Broosa, and in 1872, he returned to the United States in feeble health. But although in America, his heart was in Turkey, and although not vigorous in body, he returned in 1874 to Turkey in order to meet a call for a professor of Turkish and Greek in the Theological Seminary at Marsovan, where he arrived March, 1874. One of his fellow teachers there said of him: "I had never seen him before, but he made the same impression on me, that I suppose he made on every one—first, last and always—that of a man, good, kind, wise—a man who had seen work, and was ready for more. He was venerable in appearance, a special requisite in the East. And while the great congregations sat on the floor with face upturned toward the desk,

> How sweetly flowed the gospel sound
> From lips of gentleness and grace.

But Dr. Schneider was then beginning to fail in health. There was one year more of soldiering for him to do in Turkish soil." In the summer of 1875, he was compelled by nervous prostration, to leave Turkey, and go to Switzerland, and finally, to return to America, where he died on September 14, 1877.

He was a man of prayer. "His prayers," said his associate, Rev. Dr. Crane, "breathed the spirit of one accustomed to commune with God. Those prayers that he used to utter in that booth-like structure where hundreds gathered in the early days of his missionary labors at Aintab, still ring in the ear of memory—so urgent, so comprehensive, so full of trust in the promises, and so sympathetic in their tone to all. The same was true of his private devotions. He had his times of prayer and they were sacred. If by any means they were broken in upon, he would at his earliest opportunity return to them even though he was on horseback or in his walks. Often in his travels the time he rode was spent in prayer.

Few missionaries in any field have been permitted to labor longer, and few have left behind them, among those for whose spiritual welfare they have toiled and labored, more of grateful remembrance, than he. For more than forty years he was privileged to be connected with the work so dear to his heart, laboring in season and out of season, in every department of missionary service; in preaching, which was his delight; and in teaching young men, and preparing them for the ministry in their own land. Few have traveled more extensively than he as pioneer; few have labored in more places in Turkey; few certainly have been more willing to spend and be spent wherever they could serve their Master most acceptably; few have more cheerfully endured privations of the service, than Dr. Schneider. Wherever, at home or abroad, he was personally known, he was revered; and as long as the missions of the American Board in the Turkish Empire are cherished by American churches, so long will the name of Benjamin Schneider be honored as one of the earliest and most devoted missionaries. President Fuller, of the Aintab College, thus bears testimony to him: "His forty years of labor in the Turkish Empire, whether we consider the faith, courage, wisdom and heroic endurance displayed, or the grand results attained in the establishment of a new order of faith and living, are of monumental importance. The Protestant churches of Turkey, and especially those of the Central Turkey Mission, where so large a part of his missionary life was spent, have a deep and filial love for the memory of the man who so zealously taught, and wisely led them in the days of their early trials."

Chapter X.

SAMUEL M. ZWEMER.

Arabia, too, has been receiving the gospel at the hands of the Reformed,—Arabia which gave the law of Moses and the prophet Mohammed to the world, has now heard the gospel of Jesus Christ. The Theological Seminary of the Dutch Reformed Church at New Brunswick, New Jersey, had as one of its professors in the eighth decade of the nineteenth century Rev. John G. Lansing, a son of the honored missionary of the United Presbyterian Church in Egypt, Rev. Julian Lansing, D.D. The latter had been praying for many years for Arabia, and his enthusiasm for the regeneration of that land by the gospel finally brought forth its fruit in his son. Through the influence of the latter, three students of that Theological school decided to go to Arabia, Samuel M. Zwemer, James Cantine and Philip T. Phelps.

They made application to the Board of Foreign Missions of the Reformed Dutch Church under whose auspices they had been educated. But that Board felt itself at the time too heavily burdened by a debt of $35,000 to enter on work in a new field of missions. However the attention of that church had been called to this movement and contributions began to come in. The young men, too, determined to go, without the support of their Foreign Board, relying on private subscriptions and prayer. An undenominational missionary society was organized August 1, 1889.

A few days later Dr. Lansing composed the Arabian Mission hymn which has been a great inspiration to these workers in Arabia.

> "There is a land long since neglected,
> There is a people still rejected,
> But of truth and grace elected,
>   In his love for them.
>
> Softer than their night winds fleeting,
> Richer than their starry tenting,
> Stronger than their sands protecting,
>   Is his love for them.
>
> To the host of Islam leading,
> To the slave in bondage bleeding,
> To the desert-dweller pleading,
>   Bring his love to them.
>
> Through the promise on God's pages,
> Through his work in history's stages,
> Through the cross that crowns the ages,
>   Show his love to them.
>
> With the prayer that still availeth,
> With the power that prevaileth,
> With the love that never faileth,
>   Tell his love to them.
>
> Till the desert sons now aliens,
> Till its tribes and their dominions,
> Till Arabia's raptured millions,
>   **Praise this love of them.**

The Reformed Church.

Rev. James Cantine sailed October 16, 1899, and Rev. Mr. Zwemer on June 18, 1890. They met at Aden, Mr. Cantine going to Muscat, to the Persian gulf and Bagdad, while Mr. Zwemer went south along the coast, accompanied by Kamil, and landed at Busrah.

The story of Kamil is of fascinating interest and reveals a life entirely surrendered to Christ, even to death. On the morning of February 10, 1890, a young Syrian called on Rev. Dr. Jessup, the well known Presbyterian missionary at Beirout. He told the story that he had met a Maronite priest near Beirout who advised him to go to the Jesuit college, which he did. One of them gave him an Arabic Testament. But his father caught him reading it and burned it in the kitchen fire. The next day one of the Jesuits gave him another New Testament and suggested he adopt a false subterfuge to his father so as to be able to retain it,—that he tell his father that he had bought it in order to write a tract against it, which was a clear untruth. It was the old Jesuit policy that the end justifies the means, however wicked the latter might be. But the mind of the pure-minded Syrian revolted against such sinful trickery and replied: "What! advise me to lie to my father! Never!" He laid down his book and came away. The Jesuits had proposed to send him to Alexandria, Egypt, for education, but his family protested.

So he left the Jesuits disgusted, after being with them a month, and came to Dr. Jessup, saying: "I am not at rest, I find nothing in the Koran to show one how God can be just and yet pardon a sinner." Dr. Jessup allowed him to come and read the Bible at his house. He seemed instinctively to learn the way to Christ, so quickly he grasped it and was soon rejoicing in the felt forgiveness of his sins. He proved to be a true Nathaniel without guile. He entered the mission school at Suk in Syria to prepare himself for work among the Arabs. Being afraid for his life if he returned to Beirout, he spent the summer of 1890 in evangelistic work among the Bedouin. After having been a Christian only seven months he was found trying to convert no less a man than the Greek bishop, who so admired his abilities and zeal that he offered him a fine position. After this Kamil was baptized January 15, 1891.

It happened that Messrs. Cantine and Zwemer, of the new Arabian Mission, were spending some time at Beirout when his baptism took place. They requested the services of Kamil, which was the more willingly granted because, as he was a convert from Mohammedanism, his life was to some extent always in jeopardy in that region. He arrived at Aden February 7, 1891. He at once set to work among the Mohammedan merchant caravans that passed through Aden. His knowledge of Mohammedanism enabled him to interest and answer his listeners. He was so successful that he frequently had fifty to one hundred seated around him listening to the Bible.

He then accompanied Mr. Zwemer along the coast of the Red Sea southward. At Mejada they ran their boat ashore owing to the storm. When they had drawn the boat up on the beech and were preparing some food, an armed Bedouin came up with a long spear and warned them against being robbed or killed. They said they feared nothing as God was with them. But in five minutes another Bedouin rode up and demanded coffee and finally money, which was refused. Then a crowd of Bedouin women and children came down upon them. It was difficult to protect their goods. Sometimes a child seized one thing and a woman another and four or five at once reached out their hands. They seized the boat and refused to let them launch again. The missionaries then demanded their help and all laid hold and drew the boat to the water. Mr. Zwemer then went up to the chief robber and cut off a little bead hanging from his neck as a keepsake. The latter never uttered a word. He then gave him a cup as a keepsake, and gave them all medicine for their ailments. The missionaries then took their spears and stuck their shafts into the ground. He then offered prayer, praying for half an hour and exhorted them, closing the prayer in the name of Jesus, to which all the company responded "Amen! and Amen!" And they exclaimed: "Never in all our lives will we cut off the roads, rob them on the highway again, or speak harshly to a stranger." And on parting they said: "Go in peace."

Kamil continued preaching to the sailors of boats at Aden and in the bazaars there. He wrote earnestly to his father, trying to open his eyes to the truth in Christ. The father replied and the correspondence resulted in a bitter controversy. Kamil also itinerated in the neighborhood of Mecca, the centre of Mohammedanism of the world. He went from Aden to Busrah in January, 1892, with the mission. His last letter is dated April 22, 1892, where he says Mr. Zwemer had urged him to go boldly into the Mohammedan coffeehouses and preach Christ, but he felt it would be unwise as there was no religious liberty there as at Aden where they were under the British flag.

But he busied himself, although sick, with personal conversations and with Bible distribution. On May 22 he had visits from twenty-three Mohammedans, five Christians and one Jew, and sold two Bibles. He died suddenly June 24, 1892, probably of poisoning. The Mohammedans sealed the house where he stayed, thus preventing any investigations. They buried him with Mohammedan burial in spite of the protests of Mr. Zwemer that he was a Christian, which made it suspicious that they had led to his poisoning; for his rapid burial was contrary to their long drawn out rites of burial. Even the place of his burial was sealed. So died a bright spirit after a two years' ministry for Christ. But we doubt not that the results of his ministry will remain. If Henry Martyn's brief stay in Persia nearly a hundred years before, led to results which appeared a half century later, we believe Kamil's testimony will yet reveal similar results.

But difficulties arose to the mission. Besides the

poisoning of Kamil, another of the converts was arrested. The money received by the Home Committee lessened on account of the illness of Rev. Prof. Lansing, at New Brunswick, who had been the godfather of the mission. Cholera came and interfered with their work in Arabia. Still there was also encouragement; for new missionaries were sent out, as Peter J. Zwemer and James T. Wycoff, M. D., but the latter, though the third of the medical missionaries sent out, was soon compelled to return by ill health.

Still results began to show themselves although the field was very hard. After laboring from 1892-99, during which time their Scriptures sales arose from 1,620 in 1892 to 2,464 in 1899, they at last gained their first convert. A soldier at Amara accepted Christ and came to Busrah for instruction. He had suffered the loss of all things, but witnessed a good confession wherever he had been dragged as an exile or driven as an apostate. Another convert was a middle-aged Persian, who was deeply convicted of sin by reading a copy of Luke's gospel in the dispensary at Busrah.

Perhaps the most interesting feature of their work was the school opened at Muscat by Peter J.

Zwemer for eighteen orphan slave boys who had been rescued from slavery in Africa and were handed over to the mission. The medical work also began to tell, as among the Mohammedans there are no doctors. Mr. Peter J. Zwemer died October 18, 1898, after heroically fighting with repeated attacks of fever there, until driven home to die. But in dying his heart was still in Arabia, for his last letter to his parents said he had just secured $100 for a Muscat touring boat. Thus the Lord has already blessed this new mission with martyrs. They will be the seed of the Arabian Church, the forerunners of many saved.

Mr. Samuel M. Zwemer is still laboring for the salvation of Arabia and greatly instructing and influencing the churches at home by his books "Arabia" and "Raymund Lull," who was the first great missionary to the Mohammedans, preaching to them during the Middle Ages.

BOOK IV.

THE REFORMED IN THE EAST INDIES

Chapter I.

JAN KAM, THE APOSTLE OF THE MOLUCCAS.

THE East Indies had Protestant missions early. The Dutch East India Society sent the gospel to these heathen lands very early, so that by 1772, it is said, there were 100,000 converts on the island of Java, and by the end of the seventeenth century, 40,000 in Amboyna. But the work was very superficially done, and many of the converts secretly clung to their old heathenish superstitions and were only Christians in name. It was left for this century to really begin the mission work of the East Indies on a new basis and with a true missionary method, so that it is now done more thoroughly. It was the subject of this sketch who gave the great impulse to this forward movement, especially on the Molucca or Spice Islands. This group of islands is named thus because of its beautiful nutmeg tree with its deep green, glossy leaves and evergreen aromatic flower buds called cloves.

The Molucca Islands were first captured by the Portuguese, but taken from them by the Dutch in

1580. The Dutch cruelly oppressed the people, ordering all the spice trees to be cut down on all the islands, except Amboyna.

The first attempt in the nineteenth century to revive the mission work in Amboyna was by Jabez Carey, a son of William Carey, the great missionary to India. Amboyna was captured from the Dutch by the English. William Carey issued an appeal for the island, which for ten years had had no missionary, although twenty thousand of its forty-five thousand inhabitants were already nominal Christians. And the first one to respond to this call was his own son. This son had been a source of special anxiety to his father. The remarkable story is told that at an annual meeting in London the Baptist minister, Dr. Ryland, preached in the Dutch church. He praised the good fortune of William Carey, who had two sons in the missionary field. "But," he continued, "there is a third son who gives him great concern in that he has not yet found the Lord." Then, after a long pause, during which many tears came to his eyes, he lifted his voice, saying: "Brethren, let us send up to God a united and earnest prayer for the conversion of the third son, Jabez." For two minutes the great assembly of two thousand persons, was in silent prayer. In one of the first letters received by them, Jabez's conversion was announced at almost the very time when the great assembly was praying for him. He then went to Amboyna in 1814. He wrote that there were many villages nominally Christian, each village having its church with a school and schoolmaster, and a place for a minister. He found on closer examination that the churches were largely attended. He tried to improve the schools and get the natives to give up idolatry. Carey's activity gave hope of great results. But when the islands were given back to Holland in 1815, he was compelled to leave, as the Dutch government would not allow any foreign missionary of another nation there.

In his place, however, came a man who possessed all his spirit—yes, the missionary spirit of his greater father, William Carey—Jan Kam. For the Netherlands Missionary Society which had been organized in Holland, after doing some work in South Africa, now listened to the calls from the Dutch provinces in the East Indies and sent a number of excellent missionaries. Among these was the pious and devoted Jan Kam. He was born at Herzogenbosch in 1770. His love for missions was awakened by his contact with the pious Moravians at Zeist. In 1811 he gave up his position as court messenger of justice, so as to go to Rotterdam and prepare himself to become a missionary. His preparation as a missionary was made partly at Rotterdam, partly at Zeist. He was sent out by the London Missionary Society in 1812, arriving at Surabeya May, 1814, where he spent seven months. Later he became a Dutch chaplain at Amboyna.

When he arrived at Amboyna (1815), he was gladly received, and preached his first sermon (March 5th) on John 17:3, "And this is life eternal, that they might know thee, the only true God, and Jesus Christ, whom thou hast sent." He came truly to bring eternal life to many on these islands. Although the regularly appointed Dutch minister at Amboyna, his heart was in missionary work. When he preached in Dutch, his congregation numbered one thousand, and when he preached in Malay, it numbered six hundred. His congregations soon doubled. But his heart went out for the heathen around, and especially for the natives, who had been nominally converted to Christianity, and who were scattered as sheep that have no shepherd. He found them very low in piety. Their condition can be inferred when we remember that a Bible was so rare that one sold for forty-eight dollars. So sad was their condition that he said there are thousands here who would give all their property for a Malay Bible.

Kam also began devotional meetings in his house (which held from three to four hundred persons), so as to prepare them for the communion. He then traveled everywhere, baptizing the people, who had so long been without a minister. He says that from March to May he baptized three thousand children of ten years old and under, because there had been no Dutch minister to do this for so many years, and the children had grown up without baptism, although waiting to be baptized. He began devotional meetings in twenty-seven villages for the heathen, which were largely attended.

His services were soon interrupted by an earthquake. One Sunday morning in April, at five A. M., there was a very severe earthquake. "My house," he says, "was so shaken that my books were thrown on the floor from their case. Many people fled with nothing but their night garments, out into the open fields for safety. This shock was soon followed by a second. This continued until the island was shaken for six days. Twice during church service was the church shaken, and this caused not a little alarm among the congregation. But I took my refuge in prayer to God, and speaking on Psalm 46, 'God is our refuge,' etc., I improved the occasion by reminding them of the vanity of riches and the uncertainty of life." Before the end of the month he learned that in some of the other islands the churches had fallen in on the people, so that they had to be pulled out of the rubbish. He said: "How fortunate we were." On the second Sunday in May he began mission meetings, the Dutch governor being present to show his sympathy. Kam urged upon them very earnestly the need of a Bible Society, so as to distribute Bibles, and one was organized June 5. This Society soon raised 4,000 thalers and scattered 4,000 Malay Bibles.

He not only preached the gospel in Amboyna, but he showed his wonderful activity by preaching on the other islands. Being the only minister at that time in the Moluccas he, every year, visited the congregations in the neighboring islands. During the summer of 1815 he made a journey to the neighboring islands of Haruko, Sapama and Ceram. Haruko had 6,000 Christians and Sapama 9,000. He found in Haruko that many of the villages had sunk back into idolatry. But the earthquake had been to them a loud call of God to bring them back to repentance; and they had everywhere been burning their idols, and were only waiting for some Christian minister to come and preach the gospel to them. He, therefore, found a field prepared for the harvest. His services were attended by great crowds. He baptized many children, and received many adults into the Church, after they had confessed their penitence and made a profession of faith. He stayed with them eight days, preaching every evening, and was visited by multitudes seeking Christ. He then celebrated the Lord's Supper amid the tears of the communicants. On October 16 he left that island and came to Ceram, where a great crowd of men awaited his coming. And when he landed, they all cried out: "Welcome to our villages. Praise to God, who visits us with His salvation." Twenty years had passed since a Christian minister had been seen among them. He found, however, that unlike the inhabitants of Haruko, these had not lapsed back into idolatry, but had remained firm, and were waiting for a minister to come and baptize and administer communion. He, therefore, spent much time in baptizing their children and in preparing adults, who had grown up without baptism, for baptism. Here he found the Alvure tribe, who were of the same race as the Hottentots in Africa, and who, in their low, sunken condition, offered a wide field for missions. He preached in twelve villages of the island. When the communion came, he had to use ship crackers, as there was no bread, for they use sago and fruits, not bread, for food.

In one of the villages his life was endangered. For only two hours after his departure it was attacked by the cruel Alvures and some of the villagers killed. Then he went to the island Sapama, which had twenty-two Christian villages and a Christian population of 11,000. There he stayed three weeks. On this island he found more education and culture. He found in many places an awakening among the Christians. Although the heat had become stifling, yet his labors were unbroken and his strength was continued. The interest of the natives in his journeys was so intense that many followed him from one village to another, and even from one island to another. He returned to Amboyna, December 4, 1815. His report was that he had baptized 2,919 children at Amboyna, 1,290 at Haruko, 2,538 in Sepama, 650 adults in Ceram, and 156 adult heathen, making a total of 7,553, to which must be added 1837 baptized heathen in Amboyna and other islands, a total of 9,490. Few missionaries ever had the opportunity or the honor of doing so great a work for the Church.

Nor did he rest long. Like the Apostle Paul, he was instant in season and out of season. His active, consecrated spirit could not rest when there was so much work to be done. Being the only minister, his work in reviving these churches was very laborious. By March, 1816, he was again on his travels. This time he visited other islands—Buno and Manieke. On the former island there had been no minister for thirty years, so that the membership of the congregation had almost died out and was limited to six old persons. There were great crowds who attended his services, who, it is true, had heard the Christian religion from the schoolmasters stationed on the island, but they had never been baptized or even seen a baptism. He there baptized 200 adults and 3,000 children under twelve years. His services were greatly crowded, but there was a great scarcity of Bibles and Church books. Many could read, having been taught reading in the schools. And they considered themselves happy, if they could by chance get hold of only one page of the Bible. On his return he was very nearly shipwrecked, as the storm drove them toward the rocks, but a kind Providence made him escape in safety. In the fall of that year he again visited Haruko, where he was glad to notice an evident progress in the spiritual things. Many whom he had baptized, had become communicants. He also visited Ceram, where a man came to him from Nulalliwu, a village whose inhabitants had gone back to idolatry, and had burned their church and their Bibles. He came to ask Kam to come and preach the Gospel among them again. Kam went to them and stayed with them three days. But even before his coming they had gathered together their idols and burned them, and they had also burned the houses dedicated to the worship of devils. The idols they burned were worth two hundred and fifty thalers. Amid the tears of the congregation he preached to them of Christ; and after he was through many came forward and promised that hereafter they would never go back to idolatry again, but would remain true to God and His Word.

In the autumn of 1817 he sailed for the island of Celebes, where he found a large field among the nominal Christians, and also among the Chinese. He had hardly landed, when an Alvure chief came to him and asked him earnestly for a teacher for his village. Kam asked him why he wanted to be a Christian. "Because," he replied, "I know that the Christian religion is the best." Kam promised him a teacher, and the chief's heart was greatly stirred as he attended service in the house of the governor, where a number of adults and three Chinese, who desired to profess their faith in Christ, were baptized. He then visited the Sangir islands, where the king attended the service with his whole family, as did a great crowd of people. He then visited the island Dschian, where he found the king a very pious man. The king read the Bible daily, and rejoiced greatly to hear him preach and converse with him. He urged Kam to baptize a large number of slaves who had been instructed by a pious schoolmaster. Kam then went again to the Sangir islands, where he found the people in a still sadder condition than on the other islands. Even the school teacher had only scattered leaves of the Bible with which to teach. Instead of paper they had to use pieces of white wood on which to write. In some villages there were no schoolmasters, and the little boys read to the older persons in the churches. The poor people received him joyfully, and he had to split up his New Testament, leaving a gospel or an epistle to each church. "But what was that," he says, "among a people who needed 3,000 Bibles?" Everywhere, by the king and the people, he found a joyful hearing. On this journey he stayed so long that his friends at home gave him up as lost. When he returned to Amboyna, they streamed in crowds to his house, singing psalms of thanksgiving that his life had been spared. At which his captain wondered and said to the physician: "See how those sheep love their shepherd." In 1818 he made another trip to Haruko, Sapama and Ceram. While at Rasalout, robbers appeared in the night, for the islands were infested with pirates, but he was saved by the Dutch resident sending troops.

Kam was not only active in travelling and preaching the Gospel to the poor heathen, but also in writing home, telling the news and the needs of the mission field. His letters about his travels and his appeals to the home Church led the Netherlands Missionary Society to send out, in 1818, three more missionaries—Finn, Yung-Michael and LeBrun. The first was to remain with Kam and aid him in his twenty-eight congregations in Amboyna and the sixty on the neighboring islands, making eighty in all, while LeBrun went to the southern island of Timor, and Yung-Michael went to the twenty-two congregations at Ternati, from which he visited Celebes and the Sangir islands. The Missionary Society in Holland also sent him a printing press, so that he was now able to print Bibles and other devotional books for the people.

In 1819 Kam undertook a journey to the eastern and northeastern parts of Amboyna. Everywhere he was received with gladness, and even with the shooting of guns, so as to show their joy. The first villages had, he knew, relics of idolatry. He, therefore, hunted for the idols. And as the top of the hill, on which they were, was dangerous, he sent his companion up, who in a moment threw all the paraphernalia of idolatry over the precipice, so that the idols were broken to pieces before his eyes. Only one beautiful earthen vessel, decked with garlands of flowers, which held an offering, his companion did not want to destroy, and brought it down with him. Kam paid him for its full value, and then had it broken to pieces. He aimed to show to the congregation how wrong it was to retain any of these things. This act of his made a deep impression on all the neighboring villages, who hastened to put away idolatry. He rejoiced to scatter 4,000 Bibles, but soon found that they were not enough. They, however, awakened a great interest. Indeed, sometimes the desire to possess a Bible was so great that he could not forbear cutting up copies of the New Testament and scattering them in parts among the hungry people. In the near village of Liliboi, he says, he knew there was a chest of idols, decked in costly gilt clothes. He did not publicly speak of his desire to destroy them, but preached very earnestly on Colossians 3:1, "Ye are raised up with Christ." The next day the elders came and asked him if he did not think anything more about the idols. He said: "Bring them all to me." They were all brought to the school, packed into a sack and cast into the sea, while the people sang psalms. In 1820 he had 3,000 copies of a small catechism printed to satisfy the longings of the people for the Word.

Thus Kam, with wonderful wisdom, activity and consecration, watched over and guided the evangelization of these islands. Year after year he visited the islands, evangelizing or sending them missionaries, who were sent out from Holland. Good reports came from the mission stations to him as the results of his work. Thus, in 1821, a teacher on the island Haruko reported that the inhabitants of a village, of their own accord, cast away their idols, burning them and casting their ashes into the sea. In 1823 he visited the southwesterly islands, after he had received a hundred souls into his own congregation at Amboyna. In 1825 he visited the large island of Timor, with its more than 20,000 nominal Christian inhabitants. In 1827 he again went on his journeys to Buno and Sapama, baptizing and adding to the Church. On this trip he added 600 to the Church and administered the communion to 4,000. He founded a seminary at Amboyna, where school teachers were to be trained. In it, by 1828, he had trained 28 school teachers and sent them to the neighboring islands. This seminary became a power for the Church in later years.

But his large field proved too much for his strength. In his own charge at Amboyna he had 80 churches and 50,000 Christians, and 100 schools to superintend. The largeness of his field prevented him from doing as thorough work as he wished. But there is no question about his faithfulness and consecration. He and Vanderkemp of South Africa are the two jewels in the crown of the Reformed missions of Holland. He went thus up and down, from island to island, and from church to church, laboring in God's vineyard until he wore his life out; and in July, 1833, he died of overwork. But he had become the father of those island churches, and was looked up to by the native Christians as a father in Israel. He had well earned his title—the Apostle of the Moluccas.

His death caused great weeping and mourning throughout all those islands. He was greatly missed by the missionaries, but his labors of nearly twenty years laid the foundations of the East Indies missions again. Wherever he would go, he was looked on by the simple-hearted natives as an angel from heathen. He was, indeed, an earthly angel—a messenger to bring the Gospel to them. He was truly an Apostle Paul of the nineteenth century, "in journeyings often, in perils of waters, in perils of robbers, in perils by the heathen, in perils in the wilderness, in perils in the sea, in weariness and painfulness, in watchings often, in hunger and thirst, in fastings often, in cold and nakedness." His labors among those Spice islands made them come up before God as a sweet smelling savor; and the fragrance of his life, greater than the scent of the islands, has gone out into the ends of the earth.

Chapter II.

EMDE THE WATCHMAKER OF SURABEYA

The Island of Java—the pearl of the Dutch East Indies,—with its population of twenty-two millions, mostly Buddhists (though with some Mohammedans), has made little progress in missions. Missions were planted there very early in the 17th century, Justus Heurnius being one of the first and greatest of these early Dutch missionaries. A graduate in medicine and theology at Leyden, he wrote a book to interest his countrymen in missions in 1618, which caused a great stir, and in 1624 the East India Company sent him to Batavia, where he at once began laboring among the Malays and Chinese. His earnest evangelistic spirit led him to preach a sermon on the 82d to the 85th answers of the Heidelberg Catechism, in which he urged that the church there should become independent of the State. This brought him into collision (1632) with the governor of the East India Company, who arrested and imprisoned him. When released he left Java, in 1633, for the island of Amboyna, where he labored most earnestly among the natives. The Mohammedans were also active in missionary work there at that time, and they poisoned his food. Though he did not die yet it so weakened his system that he was finally compelled, 1638, to return to Holland. But he still labored hard to interest his countrymen in missions and before he died he had done considerable translation of the parts of the Bible into Malay. The Dutch by 1758 had the whole Bible translated into Malay. But though it is said there were 100,000 converts in Java by the end of the 17th century, yet the work had been so superficially done that little remained of the early mission, and in the 19th century Christian work in Java has been exceedingly hard, there being now, it is said, only about 12,000 converts.

But in spite of this darkness, three points of light appear in missionary work in that beautiful island, the Christian colony at Depok, the life and work of the Dutch Reformed missionary Jellesma, and the remarkable work of the layman Emde.

Depok is a town seven miles south of Batavia, which a pious merchant named Chastelein founded with his slaves in 1715. He offered to give them their freedom and the land they occupied, if they would become Christians. They did so and were baptized. A clean, beautiful village sprang up there, quite in contrast with the filthy heathen villages around. It was a little land of Goshen in the midst of the darkness of Egypt—an oasis in the desert. The Rhenish Missionary Society in 1878 established a training school for evangelists in this village. When Rev. Dr. Jessup visited it in 1893 he found a strong native church there and a theological seminary with thirty students from different parts of the East Indies,—the sons of cruel head-hunters of Borneo, of the fierce islanders of Celebes, of cannibals of Sumatra as well as of Java.

Jellesma was sent out by the Netherlands Missionary Society and labored first at Surabeya, 1848, where the government forbade him to labor outside of the town, as it did not want him to convert the heathen. As soon as permission was given him, in 1851, he laid the foundation of a seminary at Morjo-Warno (1852). By the time of his death, in 1858, in seventeen villages there were 200 Christians. On his tombstone is the inscription, "The Apostle to the Javanese." There are now 4,200 Christians in that district.

At Aroldsen, in the county of Waldeck, Germany, there was a child born in 1774, named Emde. He went to school in a neighboring village, where the schoolmaster made such a deep impression on him by his teachings, that whenever Emde would speak of him, even sixty years after in distant Java, he would take off his hat. His father taught him the trade of miller, but the family was so large that young Emde often suffered from want, so when he was sixteen years old, he left home, and, like the German apprentices, he travelled around through Hesse, Thuringia and Hanover, and finally Westphalia. But he did not like the Westphalian mills, and so returned home again. In 1801 a younger brother went to Holland as a soldier, and he went after him to hunt him up. But when he came to the Dutch border, his papers were found to be improperly made out, and he was ordered to return. As he was standing there, a Dutch courier, who had lost a servant, came down the street. Emde offered to be his servant, and was accepted. So he was allowed to remain in Holland. He continued seeking his brother, but failed to find out anything about him.

At last he became tired of Holland and felt like going to his home again. Just then, when he was dissatisfied, he happened to meet a number of sailors. They told him of a land where sugar and coffee grew, and where there was no winter, but an unending summer. He believed them when they told him about the sugar and the coffee; but to his simple mind the last statement was contrary to the Bible, and therefore could not be true, for Genesis 8:22 said summer and winter should not cease. And so he said he would not believe them. But although he did not believe them, the news disquieted him. He kept on thinking about this land of perpetual summer. His curiosity was aroused.

Finally, as he was tired of the flat lowlands of Holland and its windmills, he determined he would go to Java and see for himself whether there was a land there where there was no winter. He took a situation as a sailor on a vessel bound for Batavia. Although his pay was small, he consoled himself that that would enable him to see this strange land of summer, and he would still have thirty-six dollars in addition in his pocket. When he came to Batavia, he found that the sailors were right—that sugar and coffee grew in that paradise of earth, the island of Java; and he also found that there was no winter, only summer. How he ever harmonized it with the Bible, we do not know, but at any rate it never led him to lose faith in his Bible. Afterwards he would have liked to have returned to Europe and see again a real winter, even if it froze him blue, yet he was prevented by providential circumstances from ever seeing a snowflake again. For such a strong, healthy laborer, as he was, was just the kind that the Dutch government wanted for its navy, as the climate in the East Indies carried off those who were sickly or weak. The government therefore compelled him to enter its service, and packed him off to Borneo on a man-of-war to suppress the pirates. Here he continued so long that he would often call its inhabitants his countrymen.

Now ship-life was profligate, and with profanity and obscenity they woke up in the morning and went to bed at night. But the greater the danger, the greater was revealed Emde's nobleness. For he did not forget what the old schoolmaster said: "Call on the Lord in thy need." When his comrades saw that he prayed, they swore at him, but he kept on praying, until they nicknamed him "the praying brother." Emde was one of those who, when opposed, became only the more determined. Often he rebuked them for their sins with the natives, and when they mocked him, he only prayed the more. Thus he spent six years.

The Reformed Church. 323

One day his vessel was anchored in the Rhede before Banjarmassing. The Dutch Resident wanted to go to Tabenio, so they sailed that night, but came to Tabenio in a thick fog. The sea was very shallow there, and it was low tide. When the fog lifted, the shore was filled with pirates, who had many boats. In these they rapidly approached the bessel, which had become becalmed in a fog. They came toward her on the side where there were no cannons. When Emde saw the great danger, he cried unto his God for help, and he had great peace of soul. But the Dutch Resident on board gave up hope, and ordered the vessel to be blown up. Emde thought, however, it would be plenty of time to do that when the enemy had come on deck. He, therefore, gathered his comrades around him, and prepared to fight with the pirates. The balls flew thick. Many of his comrades fell on his right and his left. Nearer and nearer came the boats of pirates, until they were within two rudders' lengths of the ship. Suddenly, as if by accident—no, it was in answer to Emde's prayers!—a wind sprang up and filled the sails. The steersman quickly turned the ship, so that the side that had cannons was turned toward the pirates. The sailors fired a broadside, and the waves were immediately filled with overturned boats and dying pirates. For this deliverance his impious comrades considered him for a time a brave man, but they soon forgot it again. His vessel then went to Surabaya, and, as he was sick, he received permission to stay there for a while, although not allowed to leave the Dutch service. When the English conquered Java in 1811 he became free from the government's employ and located at Surabaya.

Surabaya was, next to Batavia, the largest commercial town on the island. It is beautifully situated along the river Kalimas, which divides it into two parts. On the one side of the river was the native town, where the Chinese lived in stone houses and the Japanese in bamboo huts. A large bridge across the river joined that part of the city with the Dutch town. Emde soon found a German from Westphalia who formed a strong attachment for him, as they came from the same country. This German taught him to repair watches. Emde was glad to learn this trade, for in Java there were no mills, and his trade as miller was useless to him. These two Germans lived together for a while, and at last married two sisters, who were in reality Javanese princesses. For the old Javanese nobles had become very poor, and were glad to marry their children to the Dutch. These wives were, however, both Mohammedans, for European women were scarce there.

But they had many privations. Emde had no church to attend. No man cared for the souls that were there. The Dutch were largely rationalists or gross sinners, and the poor natives were left to die in dark heathenism. It was not till 1814 that Jan Kam arrived, to his great joy. As Kam was detained there by being unable to sail, Emde and some others came to him, asking him to hold a religious service. Thus Emde started a fire that never went out. When Kam had to go away, he appointed Emde to continue the services. Right faithfully did this simple watchmaker perform his duty. He would gather the few who would come every evening. They would sing a hymn and Emde would pray, read a selection of Scripture, and explain it as well as he could. As long as only a few attended, the services met no opposition. But when they began to increase in size and influence, then they aroused opposition. The Dutch residents mocked at him, and even threw stones at him in the street, and posted up scandalous pictures of his meetings.

But he bravely kept on with his work, and God richly blessed and rewarded him. For when by and by a missionary passed through the town again, Emde had the great joy of having his wife baptized, as did his German friend also.

Finally in 1820 a Dutch minister was placed at Surabaya. But, alas, he was a rationalist, like so many in Holland then, and preached not the Gospel, but only morality. Still Emde and his friends punctually attended church, although the minister fed them on husks. Yes, sometimes Emde and his band were the only ones who were there. And after service they would go to some one of their houses, and kneel down and pray God's blessing of the word preached. On Sunday afternoons Emde would teach his own family about the Bible. But all these things were not viewed with favor by the minister, who looked on Emde as a Methodist. And, although Emde was his best friend and most faithful attendant, he caused him to be arrested as a dangerous man, and brought him before the magistrates. There Emde bravely convicted the minister, showing that he really shut out the people by his miserable sermons, and yet persecuted those who wanted to go to church. For his boldness, Emde was put in prison for a number of weeks. But though they could lock the door on him, nevertheless they could not shut his mouth. He began preaching, like Paul, to the prisoners about the love and peace of God, and so powerful was his preaching that the magistrates were afraid that what they called Methodism would break out in prison, and they were glad to let him out again. His enemies even brought complaint against him to the governor general at Batavia, but nothing more was done against him. Still all these persecutions only advertised his efforts, and his prayer meetings had unheard-of-success.

Emde owed his awakening to a missionary (Jan Kam), and as a result all missionaries were welcome to his house as they passed through, whether they were Dutch, German, American or English. He kept a small suit of rooms in his house as the prophets' chamber. Owing to his association with them, he did not find it hard to organize a missionary society at Surabaya. The society was not large, but did a great amount of good. Emde was the soul of the society. It interested itself mainly in the mission stations of missionaries who had stopped at Surabaya. They raised funds, and gave bells to the mission stations and other gifts.

Emde was an earnest soul-winner. If any one came into his jewelry shop, it was not long before he would turn the conversation to the subject of religion. And he understood how to do this in a masterly way. Thus, once a high officer of the Dutch service came to him, saying of his watch somewhat profanely: "This watch is devilishly dirty." "I will clean it," said Emde, "but it is a question which is the dirtier, your watch or your heart." And very soon he showed to the officer from the Bible that God alone could cleanse the heart, or it, uncleansed, would go to the devil. On another occasion a gentleman of rank came and wanted something repaired. Emde took the watch, when the officer happened to look up at a remembrancer on the wall. Emde quick as a flash saw his opportunity. "Do you understand what you read?" asked Emde of him. The gentleman looked at him from tip to toe, and asked suspiciously: "Do you think that I am a child that I can't read?" "Yes, truly," was Emde's reply, "I thought so, for of such is the kingdom of heaven." The gentleman left as soon as possible in a thoughtful mood.

Emde's heart went out for the Javanese natives at Surabaya. He especially began to labor among the

Lipplapen, who were the children of Dutch fathers and native mothers. These spoke the Malay language. There were some tracts in Malay, but in such a learned dialect that the ordinary man could not understand them. Emde and his friends felt their need. So they began to translate the New Testament into Malay and use it at their prayer meetings. They labored at this translation for ten years. Emde prayed and the people gave, and when the translation was finished the people had gathered sufficient money for its publication. But Emde was not satisfied with caring for children of mixed marriages. He longed to save the native Javanese too. For he had married a Javanese wife, and that race were really his relatives. The Javanese were Mohammedans, but really heathen. But how could he get the gospel to them? for he could not understand or speak their language, and he felt he was too old and too little of a linguist to learn the language.

But still he labored at it. By the aid of his wife and daughter he had tracts translated in Javanese, and also Scripture texts, which he would post up on the markets for the natives to read. At last the New Testament had been translated into Javanese by Bruckner; he greatly rejoiced. At his meetings his wife and friend, who understood Javanese, would speak to the Javanese present in their own language. But for a long time the seed sown fell on stony ground. True, the father and sister of his wife were baptized, but the Mohammedans were hard to reach. Nevertheless Emde should have the credit of being one of the first heroes of the faith to stand on the walls of the proud fort of the false prophet.

About 1840 one day an old Javanese came to his shop from a neighboring village, Wioong. He had been a priest there for twenty-four years. Emde had given him a tract some time before. Emde could not talk with him, and so had to call his wife. Through her the priest told him how he had read the tract and been deeply affected by it, and that he was willing to give up the religion of the false prophet and believe on Christ. But he desired more instruction. He was gladly instructed, and went away. When he got home, he gathered his people together at Wioong and read them the tract. His act produced a great sensation in the whole neighborhood. That a Mohammedan should become a Christian was surprising. The Javanese came in crowds to hear this converted priest. And when they asked him for further instruction, he could only send them to Emde. Emde suddenly found his house full of Javanese, who came some of them two and three days' journey. Often more than a hundred at a time would be present. This was the beginning of a great movement, which down to this day has not ended.

But difficulties arose. Those who had been awakened, desired Christian baptism. Emde could not legally baptize them, so he went to the rationalistic minister at Surabeya. But the latter only put difficulties in the way. The government said it suspected these Javanese of sordid motives, as of getting gain or position or money by becoming Christians. It also declared that it was afraid to baptize them, lest it would make the Mohammedans angry and there would be an uprising among the natives against the Dutch government. So they were refused baptism. For about five years twenty of them held together. They would come together every evening, and pray, and sing, and read the New Testament, which Emde had given them, and they would attend Emde's meetings. But their desire for the sacrament became stronger and stronger, and at last they came to the magistrates for baptism. The magistrates severely questioned them, hoping to turn them aside from their purpose. But finding they were not able to do this, they at last granted them permission. It was indeed a great and happy day for Emde, when on December 12, 1843, eighteen men, twelve women and five children of the Javanese were baptized. After that many more were baptized, until six years after they had 347 communicants and 183 baptized children.

Emde's motto of life and his chosen text was Ezekiel 36:19-38. He labored for fifty years at Surabaya (1809-1859). As he became older, his Javanese looked up to him more and more as their spiritual father. They were willing to do anything for him. Thus when some years before his death the river tore its way before his house, and the government ordered him to repair the damages, the Javanese came in crowds and did all the work for him. The early ridicule by the people had long since given way to honor.

After his death his daughter Wilhelmine continued his work, until Jellesma was sent out in 1848. Emde is an illustration of what a poor but earnest layman in God's Church can do, if he will. What a rebuke he is to so many laymen in our churches at home, who will not do or say anything for Christ.

And how wonderfully God blessed him and honored his feeble efforts in the salvation of souls. Emde will have a higher crown in heaven than many kings, for he was a true Christian nobleman, and his crown will shine forever with many stars.

Chapter III.
JOHN F. RIEDEL.

Minahassa is the pearl of Dutch missions and the crown of missions in the East Indies. Minahassa is a promontory at the extreme northeastern end of the island of Celebes, which lies east of the island of Borneo. The work of missions in Celebes was begun early by the Dutch. When the Spanish were driven out by the Dutch in 1661 a Christian congregation was founded. At the beginning of the eighteenth century there were 5,400 adherents to Christianity in Minahassa, but after the missionary fashion of that day, the work was very superficially done, as only a few of them were communicants. Then years often passed without a visit from any missionary to them. Their low condition may be imagined when one remembers that twenty-eight years elapsed without their seeing a missionary, till Rev. Mr. Kam came in 1817. It was not, therefore, till 1822 that the real work of evangelizing this peninsula began. The Netherlands Missionary Society then sent its missionaries, Lammers and Muller, to the island. But, alas! the first died two years after he arrived, and the second two years after him. Their place was, however, taken by the pious Hellendoorn, called by the people "The Pious Peter." Born at Amsterdam 1793, he had been educated at the Mission Seminary at Berkel, 1816-1819. When he arrived there, he found only three communicants. He, however, labored hard at Menado, the principal city, scattering the seed; and by prayer and preaching and opening schools, his work prospered, until when he died in 1839 he had baptized 250 adults and 1,550 children, and received 115 into Church membership.

But it was the coming of the next two missionaries, Riedel and Schwartz, which led to the quiet but complete conversion of this part of the island of Celebes, so that where there were three in Hellendoorn's time, there are now more than a hundred thousand Christian adherents. The method which they pursued to produce such great results was not street preaching, such as is practiced so successfully in India, but they did it by personal conversation. It happened that there were watchhouses everywhere, and in the leading cities there were a great many watchmen, who were called from various districts to serve in them. These watchhouses the missionaries visited very carefully, not to preach, but to talk with the men. Street preaching was not carried on at all by the Netherlands Missionary Society to which they belonged. This method of reaching them was better than to visit them in their homes, for there the missionary would have been subject to a number of hindrances, especially as the farmers were rarely at home, and in the rice season they were very busy in the field. Another great aid to the mission were the schools, which were fostered by the missionaries. When the missionaries first arrived, not an Alikure, it is said, could read, write or calculate. But the schools enabled them to get hold of the children, who, as they grew up, became the nucleus around which the mission formed. And wherever a school was founded in a village, it was not long before the parents would also come into closer contact with the mission by coming to see and hear what their own children were doing. And as the missionaries taught the children the story of the Bible, their young hearts were prepared to receive Christ as their Saviour. The missionaries, however, were very careful about receiving persons into church membership. In this they were different from the early Dutch missionaries of the previous centuries, who received them only too quickly into membership. Now the candidates for baptism had to go into training for two or three years. Then, in order to become full communicants, they were placed on probation for a while, until they revealed a proper understanding of Christian truth, and also showed a character suited to a Christian life. Undoubtedly this great care aided greatly in making the foundations of the mission permanent, and prepared for the astonishing results that followed.

On Sunday the missionary usually preached in two or three of the congregations; in the others the services were held by an evangelist or school teacher. In the afternoon catechization was held in many congregations, and also Bible readings. During the week on two or three evenings meetings for instruction would be held. On the first Monday evening of each month a mission meeting was held in most of the congregations and a missionary collection taken. The celebration of the Lord's Supper was usually two or three times a year.

Schwartz preached and labored very faithfully at Langowan, preaching and founding schools. He had to labor for twelve years with little success. It seemed as if no converts appeared. But in 1843 God's Spirit was poured out on his district, until fifteen congregations were founded, and he baptized 13,068 and received into communion 1,278 before he died in 1859.

But the most influential of the three was the subject of this sketch, John F. Riedel, Schwartz's companion. He was born at Erfurt in Germany, in 1798. There, where Luther found a Bible in a convent, he also found the truth in the Scriptures. For his father died when he was only three years old. But his grandfather, over his father's coffin, desired him to be a Christian. And his mother watched over him very carefully. Every morning and evening the Bible was read in the family, and every Sunday the children were in their place in church. A severe sickness brought him under deep conviction of sin and led him to find full forgiveness in Christ. The wish of his grandfather, when his father died, that he might become a good Christian, was fulfilled. He felt continually reminded of this, and would often go and stand before his grandfather's picture and say to himself: "Such a pious man you shall become." Although confirmed by a rationalistic preacher, yet his heart clung to the old faith, and finally this completed itself by his going to Janicke's mission school in Berlin in 1822. In 1827 Riedel, with Schwartz, left Berlin to go to Holland, and then to the East Indies, for the Netherlands Society then appointed Germans to its missions. They sailed from Holland October 30, 1829, and on July 10, 1830, they visited Emde, the pious watchmaker of Surabaya, Java. Riedel then went to Amboyna.

He continued the study of the Malay language, which he had begun during his stay in Java. In May, 1831, he sailed for Menado in Celebes, the capital of the promontory of Minahassa, to begin his life-work. Kam, the apostle of the East Indies, had now his desire fulfilled. He had long wanted to have a missionary at Celebes. The Lord granted him, as to Simeon, this desire before he died, for his death came three years later. As Riedel came in sight of the island, he said to his soul, "This is the land where I will spend my life, and, if necessary, suffer there for God's glory." When he arrived at Menado, he was received with great joy by the missionary there, Hellendoorn. He soon started for his station, Tondano, situated inland near a lake. On his way he spent a night at Tomohon. As he sat that evening on the veranda, a number of the natives gathered around his interpreter. The old schoolmaster, who had once been a soldier, came to him, saying: "Sir, I know that you have a book, out of which you have gained all your knowledge—or is it two books? The New Testament I have once seen, and read in it. But the Old Testament must be much more important, for I have heard that in it was written how the world was made. Since I have been at Java, I no longer believe in heathenism. But I would like to know how the earth and man came into being." His inquiry was a type of the seeking minds of the natives around. There was great ignorance, but at the same time great readiness to be taught. Riedel went to the house and took a Malay Bible, out of which he read the story of the creation. The old soldier greatly rejoiced to be given the Bible. Such was the ignorance of the people, and yet such was their desire for the truth. But if the schoolmaster was so ignorant, what must have been the condition of his scholars? He stands out as a type of the spiritual destitution, so common there. Of Bibles there were none, and books were so rare that the schoolmaster often saved up with great care scraps of paper, on which there was printing, so as to be able to have something with which to teach the children.

Riedel arrived at Tondano October 14, 1831. On

the first Sunday he was prepared to preach a memorized sermon to them about Christ. Alas, when Sunday came, the natives went to work in the fields as usual, and he was horrified by the Sabbath-breaking. Finally he called to one who had been baptized, and asked him: "Can you go to work on Sunday?" "Yes," he replied, "if we do not have an evil sign given us." Riedel expostulated with him. The man tried to evade his warnings by saying that he thought the day before had been Sunday, and he must go this Sunday, as his servants would be in the field, waiting for him. Riedel then appealed to him, "You want to be a Christian, and yet work on Sunday. These two do not agree. Turn around and come to church." Riedel said this with such decision of voice that the man did really turn around and come to church. Riedel began his service in the little wooden chapel. Not one-tenth of the few baptized members came to the service. The sermon was listened to rather out of curiosity. When he asked why so few came, he was answered that they did not know Sunday from any other day. Many lived in the fields, and were then gathering in their rice harvest.

Such was the unpropitious beginning of Riedel's

work there. The conditions of the Alikures were very low morally. They had a bad reputation for drunkenness, and especially for thieving, while immorality and superstition prevailed. The schoolmaster there had not learned the Alikure language, and the natives had not learned the Malay language which he spoke, so there was little teaching in the school. Riedel at once began learning the native language so as to use it. In the schools he saw that the children learned the Bible stories and also learned to sing psalms, while his wife began to gather the women and teach them on Sunday afternoon. But no sooner did results begin to show themselves than opposition arose. The devil was not going to surrender his control over the people without a struggle. The native priests made fun of those who attended her class. The sewing school for girls, however, proved so helpful that it disarmed opposition. Thus quietly the seed of the Gospel was being scattered. As the natives were afraid to visit him, he and his wife made it a point to visit them and get at their hearts by sympathy. Soon, too, some of the baptized began to become more intimate with him and his family. But heathenism still retained its power. At the heathen feasts great crowds would gather, while the little wooden church would remain comparatively empty.

Riedel was often greatly discouraged. Often he asked himself the question, "How can I reach these people?" Finally Christmas came. Then a bright thought came to him in answer to oft repeated prayer, and he said to his wife: "Christmas is coming, you must bake many cakes—the German cakes." But his good wife, although always obedient to him, declared that that would be impossible, for there was not enough flour in all Tondano. "That will not interfere," he replied, "bake rice cakes." On the day before Christmas he went to the school and invited the scholars. He made them learn Christmas hymns, so that they might sing on the occasion. The news of this soon spread abroad in the village. While his wife baked, Riedel prayed and prepared his sermon. In the evening the children came. They stood in a half-circle around Riedel. Outside of this were a great many of the natives. Riedel began to catechise the children and had them sing. The parents were surprised at the knowledge of the children. He then explained the meaning of Christmas to the people. The next day, for the first time, the little church was full, but still greater was the crowd in the afternoon at his house. His Christmas cakes were hardly enough, so greatly were they enjoyed. This giving of cakes made a sensation among the natives. It was the first act by which he began to gain their hearts, so as to win them to Christ. The next day he celebrated communion in the church, but small was the company—only his family and that of the Dutch resident, seven in all. He says: "The table was small, but all of us felt that the Lord was there." Many others were present, many of whom had never seen a Lord's Supper celebrated before. On New Year's Day the church was again pretty well filled. Riedel now began to take courage in his work; but, alas, his hopes were soon dashed to the ground. The ignorant people thought that Christ died on Christmas and rose again on New Year. They utilized New Year, not for religion, but for drunkenness. So the little church at Tondano remained empty as usual, only ten or twenty adult baptized Christians, in addition to the children of the school, coming to service.

Gradually Riedel's work began to tell, but very slowly at first. He had some medical knowledge, so that his visits to the sick gave him greater influence. Even though the church attendants were few, yet these few became regular, thus showing that they were being prepared by God's Spirit to make a public profession of Christ. After he had been there three years, he wrote somewhat more hopefully to the Netherlands Missionary Society: "Men whom I have had to speak to against superstition three years ago, now desire baptism. Those who lived in immorality, have now married. Four adult children of two of the most prominent heathen priests in this district have asked to be received into the church. An old priest, who for thirty or forty years has practiced his nefarious trade and made much money by it, has come to me and with tears in his eyes begged me not to refuse him baptism, as through it he hoped to find rest to his soul."

Riedel also began making journeys to neighboring towns, looking up the schools. In 1835 there were in these 240 boys and 20 girls. Thus Christianity began gaining power. When Christmas, 1834, came, his church was again so full that many had to stand outside. It is true that many came from curiosity or because some had the idea that, in order to be a Christian, one had to go to church on Christmas and New Year, but the rest of the year could live like a heathen. Yet in the midst of these some in the large congregation had been awakened and were truly seekers. It was not, however, till 1836 that the church attendance began greatly to increase. Before that time it had been only eighty or ninety. This year it rose from 200 to 300, so that many often had to stand outside. His house, too, became too small for the afternoon gatherings for prayer. The Sunday afternoon meetings were full of blessing. There he spoke the Alikure language, which the people understood. There he questioned the people on the sermon of the morning and added explanations. The people listened with hungry hearts, and great results began to show themselves. But as these meetings had become so large, he did not know what to do. He longed to enlarge his house, so as to have room for the meeting, but he did not have the means. Suddenly a gift of five hundred florins came from Rotterdam, and he was able to do so.

In 1837, in a letter, he speaks of his eight catechumens, among whom was the oldest and most famous of the heathen priests who had been led by sickness to feel the need of a Saviour. When Riedel was first sent for by him, he found the house full of heathen priests. But the old man declared before them all that he had cast aside his heathenism and would be a Christian. Soon the news spread abroad that the chief of the Alikures of that village had become a Christian. The natives gathered with drums, wishing him all sorts of ill luck for this act. In spite of all their efforts he remained firm. When he was baptized, it was a day long to be remembered in the mission's history. The streets were filled with natives, and so was the church. When the priest and the other catechumens knelt to be baptized, there was weeping all over the church. God's Spirit was evidently moving on the hearts of the people. The old man died three weeks later, bearing a beautiful Christian testimony. He called his family around him, many of whom were still heathen, and said: "You see how good it is to have the Lord Jesus. I am sick, yet my pains are softened. My sins are forgiven, and I look with joy at death. Yet I shall not die, for my soul will go to God." Such words his family had never heard before, for among the Alikures they never speak of death or of the grave. And when one of his family asked him what he meant by the resurrection of the dead, he referred him to the parable of the sheep and the goats in Scripture.

Another influence that began to aid Riedel was a

printing press, which, in 1837, was placed at Tomohon, not very far away. Often his heart had been pained by the remarks of the scholars: "You teach us to read, but of what use is it, because we have nothing to read." A large number of Bibles also came to hand. Great was the joy of the people at this. To buy them, some came with money, here one came with a sack of rice, there a girl with eggs, here a woman with chickens. He was compelled to build a larger church, seating eight hundred persons. Indeed the whole town began to wear a changed appearance. On Sunday none of the baptized went to work in the fields with the heathen. On the contrary, even in the season of rice harvest the baptized Christians would come up out of the rice fields in large numbers to attend the services. The day was now spent in quietness, even the stamping of rice ceasing in the early morning. "How entirely different it used to be in Tondano," said the older natives.

The harvest now began coming in. In 1841 he reports that in that year he had baptized 136 adults, children of heathen 195, and of Christians 63—total 394. In 1845 a severe earthquake produced great seriousness among the people, which led many to come into the church. In 1847 he received 200 new members into the church, so that his communicants now numbered 500; and owing to his slowness and care in receiving them, and his careful instruction of them, in fifteen years only five went astray. His work, however, began growing beyond his strength, and in 1845 he sent a request to the Netherlands Missionary Society for a helper, who, however, was not sent till five years later. The number of his hearers gradually rose until 2,000 could be counted, and in 1851 even 2,500. The little church had given place to an edifice seating 2,000 people, the largest church on the island. But as his work became more severe, he began failing under it. In 1860 his end approached. Twenty-nine years he had labored there; great had been his influence, but now his work was done. As he opened his eyes on his deathbed, he saw some of his members standing there. To them he bore his parting testimony for Christ as he said, "It is all of grace." He died October 12, 1860.

Thus passed away a most active laborer of Christ. His church register revealed that he had baptized 9,341 persons, and that he had received not less than 3,851 persons as communicants. About one-third of the Christians of Minahassa were the results of his labors. His work is only a type and picture of the work done in this whole peninsula. Thus in 1857-8 a great awakening occurred in the district Ajermadidi, by which more than 12,000 came forward for baptism. Schwartz, Riedel's companion in mission work, baptized 13,068, but admitted to the Lord's Supper, 1,278. Wilken, the successor of Schwartz at Tomohon, baptized in twenty years 7,000 persons. In 1873 of the 110,000 Alikures in Minahassa 80,000 were Christians and 14,000 communicants. They then had twelve missionaries and one hundred and forty congregations. In 1876 the report showed that they had 5,000 baptisms every year, so that of the more than 100,000 inhabitants of that part of the Celebes only a small fraction were still heathen. In the forty years between 1840 to 1880, 77,571 Alikures were baptized. The zeal and consecration of these Christians is shown by the fact that in 1865 they raised $1,974, besides thousands of guldens for church bells, etc. No book is given away to them, all buy their Bibles and religious works. For their schools they raised $1,400 a year, and they even raise money now to send the Gospel to heathen around them. The 117 schools of the mission have outgrown the twenty public schools of the government, and had 10,000 scholars in 1880. In 1893 there were 200 congregations and 125 schools. In 1868 a school was opened at Tomohon for the training of assistants to the missionaries, which has done valuable service. The whole peninsula is changed, transformed by Christianity. The natives, who used to be described as "bold, rough, drunken, given to praying to the devil," have been radically changed. This is the testimony of scientists, as well as of missionaries. Just as Charles Darwin was compelled to bear witness to the blessed results of missions by what he saw in Patagonia, so his companion in science, Wallace, bears testimony to the work of these missionaries in Minahassa. He says: "The missionaries have a right to be proud of this place. Forty years ago the land was a wilderness, the people a multitude of naked barbarians who decorated their roughly-made huts with human skulls. Out of this condition of barbarism they have risen in a short time to a certain measure of culture through the efforts of the Dutch authorities. The land is now a 'garden,' worthy of its beautiful name, Minahassa, the villages are now almost all model villages, and the huts have the appearance as if on exhibition. The streets are covered with beautiful strips of green sward and bordered by ever-blooming hedges of roses. In each village there are very beautifully laid out coffee gardens, while the inhabitants take care of acres of fields of rice. In each village there is a school, in the larger ones also a church. The people are all neatly dressed, and the leading men and school teachers can vie with well-dressed English people. No one can see these men and hear their previous condition, and can doubt that they are morally and physically higher than before." Another scientist, Dr. Bleeken, says: "The Christians have become new men. They live better, eat better and are clothed better. The cutting off of heads is done away with. Thousands read, write and can calculate. The progress of the upper classes of the schools is good. Crimes are few. They obey their superiors, labor diligently and are happy. So Christianity and civilization have gone hand in hand." This island, therefore, is an answer to the critics who have declared that Dutch and East India missions are a failure. In this pearl of missions they have been a wonderful success, and are worthy to be rated with Madagascar and the Hawaiian Islands among the modern miracles of a "nation born in a day."

BOOK V.

THE REFORMED IN AMERICA.

Chapter I.

JOHN MEGAPOLENSIS.

WE have already noticed the early effort made by the Dutch Reformed to do missionary work in South America in the seventeenth century; we now turn to the work of the Reformed in North America among the Indians.

Popular opinion makes John Eliot the first Foreign Missionary in North America to the Indians. But popular opinion is sometimes wrong. For Megapolensis preached to the Indians three or four years before Eliot preached his first sermon to the Indians in 1648 near Newton. But by that year Megapolensis' labors among them at Albany were almost over. The Reformed Church can therefore boast with a just pride not only of having had the first Protestant Foreign Missionary, but that they also had the first Foreign Missionary to the Indians in North America as well as in South America. John Eliot, the apostle to the Indians, was the greatest, but not the first missionary to them. In this blessed work he was outstripped by the Reformed. John Megapolensis was born at Koedyk, in Holland, in 1601. The original name of the family was Van Mecklenburg, for his father had come from Mecklenburg to Holland. But it was the fashion in those days to change the names into Latin, especially when persons entered a profession. So his name Van Mecklenburg was changed into Megapolensis.

The Dutch had already discovered the Hudson river, and planted their colony there, called New Amsterdam, and had sold the land to patroons, a sort of American nobility. The patroon of Rensselaerswyck, who owned the land around Albany, as he wanted a minister, engaged Megapolensis to come to America for six years at a salary of $400 and his expenses. The Classis of Amsterdam approved the call, and he came to America, the second Reformed minister to the Dutch. He was about forty years of age when he left Holland for New Amsterdam (New York) in June, 1642, and arrived at Fort Orange (Albany) in 1643. This was then nothing but a trading village, especially for furs, but the fur trade built up the Dutch commerce. Fort Orange was a wretched little fort of logs, defended by four or five pieces of cannon. Around it was the little village of Beaverswyk belonging to the patroon, consisting of thirty or forty wooden houses with thatched roofs and about a hundred inhabitants. The patroon or his agent lived in the principal house, and here a room was set aside for religious service. Here the colonists used to meet for worship, which was conducted by one of their number who offered prayer and read a sermon. However their number had so increased that they wanted a minister, and therefore their patroon had sent to Holland and gotten Megapolensis. They soon built a small church, nineteen feet wide by thirty-four long. It had a canopied pulpit, with pews for the magistrates and deacons, and nine benches for the people, and cost thirty-two dollars.

It was a day of small things, the church was small and the membership only a handful, but, says Schuyler quaintly: "Whatever the edifice lacked in size and dignity, the minister furnished in piety and ability." That was no vain compliment, for Megapolensis showed himself a man of thorough scholarship, energetic character and decided piety. His preaching soon began to exert an influence on the rough manners of the frontiersmen, and acted as a restraint on the immoralities of frontier life. He was the means of saving the life of one of the most devoted Jesuit missionaries, Father Joques, who had been captured by the Indians while ascending the St. Lawrence river. The Dutch at once sought to ransom him, but the Indians refused. The Indians at first despised his gospel, but at last began to listen, and by and by some were baptized. They then took him with them to Fort Orange. Megapolensis was the means of saving him from torture and probably death. And he also subsequently saved two other Jesuits from the same fate. Joques remained at the fort, where Megapolensis was his constant friend, who never ceased his kindness until he saw him safe on his way to New Amsterdam.

But Megapolensis did more than save lives; he aimed to save souls. And he early became deeply interested in the Mohawk Indians, who came to the fort to trade in furs. In order to be able to speak to them about Christianity and Christ, he studied their language. This was a very difficult task, for he could find no one to help him, not even the agent of the Dutch West India Company, who had lived there twenty years, so he had to make a grammar of the language himself. He wrote a book on the Mohawks, which was published at Amsterdam in 1651. In this he describes his difficulties in getting their language. He says: "This nation (the Mohawks) has a very heavy language, and I find great difficulty in learning it, so as to speak and preach to them fluently. There are no Christians who understand the language thoroughly. Those who have lived here long can hold a kind of conversation just sufficiently to carry on trade, but they do not understand the idiom of the language. I am making a vocabulary of the language, and when I am among them, I ask how things are called. Then, as they are very dumb, I sometimes cannot get an explanation of what I want. Besides what I have just mentioned, one will tell me a word in the infinitive, another in the indicative mood; one in the first person, another in the second person; one in the present, another in the perfect tense. So I stand sometimes and look, and do not know how to put it down. And as they have their declensions and conjugations, so they have their increases like the Greeks. I am sometimes as if distracted, and can not tell what to do, and there is no person to set me right. I must do all myself in order to become an Indian grammarian. When I first observed that they pronounced their words so differently, I asked the commissary of the Company what it meant, and he told me he did not know, but imagined they changed their language every two or three years. I told him it could never be that a whole nation should so generally change their language, and though he had been connected with them these twenty years, he can give me no assistance."

In the same book he also described the religious beliefs of the Indians in a very quaint way: "They are entire strangers to all religion, but they have a genius which they put in the place of God, but they do not worship or present offerings to him. They worship and present offerings to the devil. If they are unsuccessful in war, they catch a bear, which they cut in pieces, then roast and offer to the devil. Also when the weather is very hot and there comes a cooling breeze, they cry out directly, 'I thank thee, devil.' If they are sick or have a pain or soreness anywhere in their limbs, and I ask them what ails them, they say the devil sits in their body and bites them there, and they also ascribe to the devil the accidents that befall them. They have otherwise no religion. When we pray, they laugh at us. Some of them despise it thoroughly, and some, when we tell them what we do when we pray, stand astonished."

This being their belief, his heart went out for them, so that he might tell them of Jesus, who saved from the power of the devil. He learned their language, so as to be able to preach it thoroughly. But it was a day of small beginnings. He was glad when only a few of them came to service. He says in his book: "When we have a sermon, sometimes ten or twelve of them, more or less, will attend, each having in his mouth a long tobacco pipe made by himself, and will stand awhile and afterwards ask what I am doing, and what I wanted that I stood there alone and made so many words, and none of the rest might speak. I tell them that I admonished the Christians that they must not steal, or drink, or love lewdness, or murder, and they too ought not to do these things, and that I intended afterwhile to come and preach to them in their country and castles, when I am acquainted with their language. They say I do well in training the Christians, but immediately add, 'Why do so many Christians do those things?'" He was able to fulfill his desire, for on several occasions he visited their settlements for the sake of preaching to them. He was greatly respected by them and a number of them united with his church at Albany. He also interested himself in them afterwards while pastor at New Amsterdam (New York), and a number of them united with his church there.

Thus was he the first Protestant missionary in North America and the first to the Indians. Of his later life time fails to speak. Nor is it necessary, for we are especially interested in him as a missionary. At the end of his six years' engagement by the patroon, he started to go back to Holland. But Peter Stuyvesant, the governor of the colony, prevailed on him to stay, as the only other minister in the colony had just gone back to Europe. He therefore remained, and died at New Amsterdam in 1670, having been one of the most trusted consellors of the governor.

A half century passed away and these Indian tribes returned the kindness to the Reformed. In 1708, when the Reformed of the Palatinate had fled to London by the thousands, and were encamped there at Black Heath, where they lived in tents loaned by the British government, it happened that at that time some Mohawk chiefs had been taken to England, so that they might be impressed with the greatness and glory of the English kingdom and its ruler, Queen Ann. In being shown the sights of the city, they were taken to see these Palatines. The hearts of these Indians were so moved by the pitiful tale of the poor Palatines that they offered them land in their Mohawk Valley. Indeed it is said that they gave them a title to land there. These colonists afterward settled on the land so kindly given by the Indians. Thus in the providence of God the Indians by their kindness returned the kindness of the Reformed. This was the first effort of the Reformed to do missionary work in North America. It started the great movement of saving the Indians by missionary work which John Eliot followed with his grand labors. But the missionary societies of this century have capped the climax, as hundreds of Christian laborers are at work among the Indians, and the Christian converts number many thousands.

Chapter II.
GEORGE M. WEISS.

Rev. George M. Weiss, one of the earliest ministers of our Church, and the organizer of the First Reformed Church of Philadelphia, like Megapolensis, showed interest in the poor Indians, but, being unsupported by any Society, he was not able to do much. In his writings, however, he showed repeatedly his interest in their salvation. Thus the first report ever published of the condition of the German Reformed in Pennsylvania (1731), was a report which was made to the Dutch Synod of 1730, and based on information given the Synod by Weiss, who had recently arrived in Holland from Pennsylvania. In it he says: "Above all things a way is opened to make known the gospel of Jesus Christ to the heathen who as yet have not heard of it. A ground of hope is observed as to the nature and disposition of the aborigines of the land. They are upright in their conduct, faithful in their word, and particularly friendly to the Palatine Germans. The latter, having themselves been subjected to oppression, they are familiar with them and friendly, allowing them to lodge in their barns at night, finding them protection from the cold and rain by their firesides, granting them the privilege of sowing their grain within their boundaries, thus freeing them from the wild horses which otherwise consume the grain. The Palatines in this way have gained the goodwill and confidence of the Indians, so that they can travel freely and without hinderance throughout the whole land and be conducted and escorted by Indians and furnished by them with food, and if payment is offered them for it they feel hurt. What may not be hoped for when a regular ministry shall be instituted among them and the gospel preached to them.*

Rev. Mr. Weiss, after having been pastor of the First Reformed Church of Philadelphia, was called to New York State, and, after doing pastoral work along the Hudson, was called to be pastor of a German Reformed Church on the borders, up the Mohawk river, at Burnetsfield, near Herkimer, N. Y. That was a new trading station between Oswego, in the northwest and Albany. In 1723 the Indians passed through there in fifty-seven canoes, loaded with 738 packs of beaver and deer skins. The first

---

*Rev. Mr. Schlatter also makes an appeal for the Indian Missions in his appeal to the Dutch and German Churches in 1752, referring especially to the work of John Eliot among the Indians and his wonderful success. But Schlatter had no opportunity to do work among the Indians directly as he was not stationed near them.

German Palatines settled there in 1723, thirty families. The centre of this Burnetsfield patent was Fort Herkimer, which was located south of the Mohawk, just opposite where the Canada Creek flows into the Mohawk from the north. Near this point the pious Germans built a school-house of logs as a place of worship. This log school-house was the church where Weiss preached when pastor of this church in the wilderness. His most prominent parishioner was the father of General Nicolas Herkimer, and the General when a young man was an attendant. Weiss was pastor there from 1736 to 1742. On May 10, 1741, he writes to the Classis of Amsterdam in Holland, saying that he will give to them a faithful description of the Indian in North America, which he had composed from his own experience with them and also a painting of an Indian man and woman, so as to give them a better idea of the Indians. On July 4, 1741, he wrote another letter, saying: "I take the liberty to report to you, in the most obedient manner, that I have had sufficient opportunity to observe the ways of the Indians, also that I have, as much as I could, interested myself in them. And, since the Indian language is unknown to me, I have employed an interpreter on several occasions and caused the most essential parts of our Christian religion to be spoken to them and have in consequence baptized several of them at their own desire. It is to be wondered at that in this country people do not insist on the conversion of the Indians. I know of only one English preacher who has interested himself to a partial degree in the Indians and urges their conversion with all earnestness. (The most of the Indians are allowed to run along without instruction, like animals.) The French of Canada are of quite a different feeling and erect churches and schoolhouses for their conversion. They thus win the affection of the Indian, which serves as a means in time of war of doing great injury to the English. From this much difficulty is to be apprehended at the present time."

The Classis of Amsterdam states at its meeting of September 10, 1742, that it had received the package containing Weiss' book and paintings. And they give in their minutes the name of his work in full, "A description of the Wild Men in North America, as to their persons, properties, nations, languages, names, houses, dress, household implements, housekeeping, hunting, fishing, fighting, superstitions, political government, besides other remarkable matters composed from personal experience by George Michael Weiss, V. D. M. It contained ninety-six pages, with a preface, and was signed by him at Burnsetfield October 4, 1741. He later returned to Pennsylvania and was not able to continue his work among the Indians.

CHAPTER III.

THE MISSION TO THE WINNEBAGOES.

The Sheboygan Classis of the Synod of the Northwest has for years been carrying on a mission among the Winnebagoes of the State of Wisconsin. This tribe had been placed by the United States Government on a reservation in Nebraska. But, becoming dissatisfied, they returned without the Government's permission, to their old home and they settled at Battle Creek Falls, Wis. As a result they became extremely poor. The Government, because of their disobedience, deprived them of ammunition. As they were dependent on game, this reduced them to such poverty that some of them had to subsist on roots, while others begged of the whites, a few being able to find work at saw-mills. When they were in this condition, they were visited by Rev. Jacob Hauser, one of the German ministers. He had visited the Oneidas, but found they had a Protestant missionary, and also the Menomonees, who had a Catholic priest, but when he came to the Winnebagoes, he found they had neither.

In the cabin of Black Hawk a council was held, at which, beside Black Hawk and Winnoshick, who were chiefs, twelve others were present. The former said, through an interpreter, that the Indians desired a school and would be glad for a missionary to teach them the word of the Great Spirit. So the Sheboygan Classis appointed a Committee on this Mission, and Rev. Jacob Hauser was chosen as the missionary. On December 30, 1878, he established the mission by opening a day school. It was held in an old log hut built by the Indians long before any missionaries were sent to them. There the interpreter, a half breed, had taught school, but had been compelled to give it up on account of lack of funds. The missionary at first lived at Black River Falls and walked four miles four days a week in order to teach them. A year after Black Hawk took pity on him and loaned him a pony, so that he could ride. He preached his first sermon to the Indians January 5, 1879. His text was John 1:29, "Behold the Lamb of God that taketh away the sin of the world." He preached it in English and it was interpreted by the interpreter. But, after preaching thus for some time through an interpreter, he gave it up, especially as the interpreter demanded too much money, and because he discovered, as he was now rapidly learning the language, that the interpreter, who was a Catholic, was putting the Catholic inter-interpretation on some doctrines. So he concluded to stop preaching until he was able to preach himself in their language. Still this was a difficult task, as the language had to be learned by hearing, having never been written. He, therefore, limited himself to the study of the language, to teaching and visiting the Indians in their homes. In 1880 a dwelling house was erected in the mission by the missionary committee, the county donating the ground. As the old schoolhouse was now so dilapidated as to be an insufficient protection against rain and cold, a chapel was built two years later, which could also be used for a school house. About that time Congress again granted these Indians their annuities and they had frame houses erected for themselves. Before that they had lived in wigwams. Now some live in wigwams and some in houses. Of the forty acres belonging to the mission, seven are cleared and cultivated, so that the Indians may be encouraged to go into farming, and thus support themselves.

In 1884 Rev. Mr. Hauser resigned and Rev. J. Stucki, who had been his assistant, was chosen as his successor. For fifteen years he labored without any conversions. During that time church services were regularly held and attended by the Indians. The school was regularly taught, and finally the good seed brought forth fruit,—John Stacy was baptized (1898) and became assistant to Mr. Stucki. On May 21, Mr. Stucki baptized George Low, his wife and five children. Five days later one of the girls of the family, a consumptive, died, and was laid to rest. The poor family were not only bowed by grief, but despised by their relatives. The child had scarcely been buried before the grandmother began to wail and mourn that the father was to blame for her death, which was caused by his becoming a Christian. This George Low had been a medicine man of the tribe and his conversion caused a sensation. It was his child's sickness that finally brought him to a decision, although his wife had been wanting to become a Christian for some time. There are now six communicants, in all there being fifteen baptized. The outlook is not very hopeful at present, as the Government school has been attracting the children from the Mission school, which had at one time ninety-three pupils.

Chapter IV.

THE INDIAN MISSION IN OKLAHOMA.

This has been the work of the gradual leadings of God's Providence. In 1895 Rev. Frank H. Wright first visited the Apache Indians of this territory. This tribe, after rebelling in 1885 under Geronimo, finally surrendered (1887) to General Miles. They were first located at Fort Sill in 1894 in twelve small villages, numbering about 260. For five years the children were sent to the Catholic boarding school Anadarko. The young men and women who desired an education were sent East, but on their return they fell back to their old life, as they had no one to help them to better ways. Rev. Mr. Wright tried to aid them, but at first failed to get the government to do so. The Government, however, in 1895 gave the land for the erection of a church and other necessary buildings and the Colombian Memorial Church was dedicated November 15, 1896, the congregation being organized that day with 22 members and the Sunday-school beginning with over 100.

In 1899 the Dutch Reformed Church formally

organized the work under its Home Mission Board. At Fort Sill it has a school of thirty-three children, and fifty-nine of the Indians have been received into the church, the Sunday-school having an average attendance of fifty. One class is composed of the Comanche Indians and is taught by Tocsi, a girl of the school, who interprets to them. Besides Mr. Wright, there are four lady teachers. An orphanage was opened at Fort Sill October 22, 1902, with sixteen children, of whom two were Comanches, the rest being Apaches.

At Colony Rev. Walter C. Roe and Mrs. Roe are missionaries and Miss Jensen matron of the Mohonk Lodge, who labor among the 125 children in the Government school, who had received no religious instruction until this mission was established. These Indians are the Arapahoes and Cheyennes. Mohonk Lodge is a shelter for the sick. Twenty-seven Indians here, including two chiefs, have become Christians and 119 have been received into membership. There are 130 in the Sunday-school.

This work among the Indians led to work among the whites, because they were so destitute of religious privileges. In 1900 four theological students went to Oklahoma to do mission work. They lived in tents, travelling in wagons, holding services by singing and preaching the gospel. This movement became so important that they agreed to return the second summer. There are now four organized churches for the whites—at Liberty, Cordell, Harrison, and Arapahoe, and six commissioned missionaries.

BOOK VI.

THE REFORMED AMONG THE JEWS.
CHAPTER I.
THE WONDERFUL MISSION AT BUDA-PESTH.

MISSIONARY work among the Jews has been lamentably neglected by the Christian Church. Yet to the Jews we owe our Saviour, and one of the signs of our Lord's return to earth is the conversion of the Jews. The Reformed Church has shared with other denominations in this neglect. And yet she has not been entirely forgetful of her duty—indeed she has done more than has generally been supposed. She has repeatedly been an important link in some of the most important movements to save the Jews. In this article we propose to give an interesting chapter of this.

In 1838 the Presbyterian Church of Scotland sent a committee of ministers to Palestine to inquire into starting a mission there among the Jews. They did not know, what missionaries now know, that there is no harder mission field in the world than Palestine. A providence turned their attention to a much more promising district in Hungary, where there are many Jews. Small events make great providences. One of the Scotch committee, Rev.

Dr. Black, fell off his camel. Rev. Dr. Bonar afterwards jocosely asked Rev. Dr. Guthrie, who was one of the committee: "What kind of an impression did Dr. Black make on the sand when he fell?" As to his mark on the sand we know nothing, but that fall left its impression on distant Hungary in a wonderful movement among the Jews. For the effect of that fall proved so serious to Dr. Black that the Scotch committee returned home. On their way they stopped at Pesth, the capital of Hungary, where one of them, Rev. Dr. Keith, was taken so sick that it was thought he would die.

And now appears another strange coincidence of providence. The first providence had been the fall from a camel, the second was the waking dream of a woman, like Pilate's wife. The wife of the Viceroy of Hungary happened at that time to be a Protestant, although he was a Catholic. The death of her dear son had led her to the Bible, and "in the Bible she met with Jesus." She then became deeply anxious for the spiritual welfare of her land. She felt in that Catholic land as if she were alone as a witness for God—"a sparrow on the housetop." From her palace she looked down on the city of Pesth below her, with its 100,000 population, and for seven years she prayed, sometimes in an agony of the spirit. Strange to say, for two weeks before Dr. Keith arrived, she invariably awoke every night (except once) at midnight, with the strong conviction that something was about to happen to her. Then she heard that a Protestant minister was dying at a hotel in Pesth. "This is what was to happen to me," she said. She sought him out and ministered to him as tenderly, as if he belonged to her own family. He finally recovered, and during his convalescence she made known to him the condition of the many Jews in her land. She begged him to get his Church to send a missionary to them, and gave her promise that she would protect the mission to the extent of her power. So the Scotch Presbyterian Church, in 1841, sent Rev. Dr. Duncan, a learned minister, and later Professor of Hebrew, as its first missionary to Pesth. This mission has had a wonderful history. It has led to prominent conversions, as Saphir (the elder) and Lichtenstein. It brought to Christ some who afterwards became prominent, as Edersheim. It has had a wonderful effect on the old Reformed Church of Hungary in strengthening the evangelical party in that Church.

Soon after the mission was opened, it was noticed

that Adolph Saphir, the most learned Jew in Hungary, a bosom friend of the chief rabbi, and a man of undoubted integrity—a modern Gamaliel—was attending the service. He came in order to learn English, but soon he learned something better—Jesus Christ. With him and led by him came his little son Adolph, an exceedingly precocious boy of about eleven years of age. One day, after they together had attended the service for some time, young Adolph, who had become seriously impressed by Christianity, asked permission to be allowed to say grace at the meal. Great was the consternation in the family and in the Jewish settlement, when he offered the prayer in the name of Jesus. Nor did he stop there. He was soon explaining the Scriptures in the Jewish quarter. Before another year had passed, he had publicly professed Christ, and was followed by his father. The conversion of so prominent a man as the father could not fail to make an impression. The Jews became very angry and compelled him to resign as director of the Jewish Seminary, and expelled him from the synagogue. His high character silenced many opponents, but still he suffered much persecution. Very soon after, the mother was convinced that Jesus was the Messiah, although she was perplexed for a while by fear of temporal losses if she became a Christian. The father delayed baptism quite a while after he found Christ, waiting and hoping that his whole family would follow him into the Church.

Finally they were ready to unite with the Church, but how could it be done? They were converted by the Presbyterian missionaries, but the Presbyterian Church was not recognized by the laws of Hungary, and no one could join it. What was to be done? Then it was that the Reformed Church stood in the breach, and opened the way by which some of the most prominent men were received from Judaism into Christianity. For the Hungarian Reformed Church was recognized by law. It numbers now two millions, but it has been hampered by the oppressing influences of Romanism, and in some parts honeycombed by the blighting influences of Rationalism. But it had as one of its superintendents and pastors Rev. Paul Torok, who was evangelical and a very warm friend of the missionary work among the Jews. The Presbyterian missionaries felt in very close and warm sympathy with the Reformed, and so, when their converts could not legally join the Presbyterian Church, they urged them to join the

Reformed. Rev. Mr. Torok gladly agreed to this. On April 4th he baptized Philip Saphir, young Adolph's brother, and on June 7, 1843, he baptized the Saphir family, father, mother, son (Adolph), and three daughters, in the Reformed church at Pesth. Before the baptism the father delivered an address, in which he described his conversion through the Holy Spirit to Christ. He bore his testimony to the change that had been effected in his wife and children, such a testimony as had not been borne in Pesth since the Reformation. The large Reformed church contained an attentive audience, and many, both Jews and Christians, were moved to tears by the address. Then, when the family were baptized by Rev. Mr. Torok, a holy awe fell on the assembly.

The Reformed Church continued for a long time to be the nurse and protector of this mission to the Jews. Many were the Jews baptized in her, for within a year thirty-five Jews were baptized there. And for her fostering care she has been richly repaid. The influence of this mission was rapidly felt in this church. The evangelical party in it rapidly increased. In helping to save the Jews, they saved themselves. Among the many notable converts from Judaism who were baptized by Pastor Torok, there were three to whom we will especially refer. The first is the little boy Adolph Saphir. He soon became a boy missionary—a fit example for every Reformed boy. Soon after his conversion he visited a Jewess, who was a neighbor. He spoke to her about her soul. He told her how happy his father's family was in having accepted Jesus. And then he finished his conversation by kneeling in prayer for her. It was felt that young Adolph was fitted to become an evangelist. And although his father looked on him as his Benjamin—the pet son of his old age, yet he willingly gave him up in early boyhood to be trained for the work of the ministry. He was, therefore, sent in the autumn of 1843 to Edinburgh. The next year he went to Berlin, where he lived with his brother-in-law, Rev. Charles Schwartz, who was a missionary to the Jews. In 1848 he returned to Scotland, where he completed his education, and was ordained at Belfast in 1854 as a missionary to the Jews. He began his work at Hamburg, but after laboring among the Jews there for a year, he resigned, because he disagreed with the society who employed him as to the method of work. He returned to Scotland, preached to the Germans at Glasgow, and then became pastor of the Presbyterian Church of South Shields, Greenwich, and afterward at London, where, after a useful and successful ministry, he died 1891. He was a prince of preachers, a modern Apollos, mighty in the Scriptures. His books, among them "The Divine Unity of Scripture," reveal his depth of thought and range of learning.

A convert better known to us in America was Alfred Edersheim. He was attending the University of Pesth in 1847. He had been reared luxuriantly in Vienna, and was a leader of fashion. He was highly educated, speaking seven languages. When the head of the bar of France, Cremeaux, visited Vienna, the synagogue presented him with an address, and young Edersheim was appointed to deliver it. Cremeaux was so pleased with his eloquence that he offered his father to take the son to Paris and provide for him, but his parents would not consent. While Alfred was at Pesth, his tutor, who spoke English, introduced him to the Presbyterian missionaries. And when the tutor left for a six months' course in an Italian university, what did he do but bring Alfred to Mr. Wingate, one of the missionaries, saying: "I give you charge of Alfred, take care of him." "How can you, a Jew," said Mr. Wingate, "give your pupil to me? You know I can only pray that he may become a true Christian." "Never mind," was the reply, "I know no one who will so conscientiously care for him." Before the six months were over, young Edersheim, under the influence of the missionaries, had come under conviction by the Holy Spirit and was led to see the divinity of Christ. He believed on Christ as his sacrifice for sin. He at once opened a class to teach English to the Jews, on the condition, however, that the Bible should be the text book. He was baptized in the Reformed Church of Pesth. Dr. Duncan says of him and of his companion convert Tomory that in the freshness of their first love to Christ, they used to read day after day the epistles of Paul, as if they had been letters that had come by that morning's mail. Edersheim went to Edinburgh to complete his theological studies. He then became a missionary to the Jews in Roumania, and then pastor at Aberdeen, Scotland. His health failing, he went to Torquay. He went to the best hotel, but finding it beyond his means, he called the landlord and asked for his bill. The landlord, who was an earnest Christian, told him to leave that with him. Meanwhile it became known that he was at the hotel, and a deputation came and asked that he might preach in a room in the hotel. Here a beautiful church was built for him, and his ministry was blessed to the salvation of many. He then entered the Episcopalian Church of England, where his fame as a preacher gave him signal opportunities. He was probably the only Hebrew-Christian clergyman ever invited by Dean Stanley to preach in Westminster Abbey. He died in 1889. It was his "Life of Jesus the Messiah" that has made him famous—the most scholarly life of Christ that has yet appeared by an English writer. And yet, with all its scholarship, it is filled with peculiar unction. A Jew himself, he threw all the intensity of his nature and race into it, as a tribute from a Jew to the Jew of Nazareth. In it with a master hand he depicts Jesus as the divine Jew and the Saviour of mankind.

Less well known, but more tenderly interesting, was the life of Philip, Adolph Saphir's brother. His was one of the most saintly young lives that the Reformed Church has ever revealed. Philip was older than Adolph and had tasted the sinful pleasures of a wild and careless life before Christianity came to him. He, however, tried through the power of dead, formal Judaism to reform, but he felt that his religion was hypocritical. In 1842 Rev. C. Schwartz visited Pesth and preached to the Jews with great impressiveness. Among his listeners was Phillip, then 19 years of age. He was deeply impressed and became a changed young man. On Tuesday, April 4, 1843, he was baptized by Pastor Torok in the Pesth Reformed Church. He was the first of the converts to be baptized, as he was going away to school, and his baptism was desired before his departure. His father and brother Adolph had already become Christians, but the father, as we have seen, delayed baptism, hoping to bring his whole family with him into the Church. So Philip was baptized alone, and two days after he wrote to Rev. Mr. Schwartz: "Tuesday was the most important day of my life. I was admitted into the Church of Christ. I can not describe my feelings to you. Ah, the infinite love of God! He has given me much peace. Nothing will deprive me of it. I praise Christ every hour. I regard my life only as a single point, and have death continually in view; therefore I lay myself into Christ's arms every evening, so that if it should be my last sleep, I may fall asleep in the Lord." Such consecration was the key to his life. He went to Carlsruhe in Germany to be trained as a teacher, but became sick and returned to Pesth two years later. But in spite of his sickness, he would not cease laboring for Christ. He organized what might be called a Young Men's Christian Association. This prospered greatly, held Bible meetings Sundays and Thursdays, and raised during the first year one hundred dollars. He also began gathering the children around his sickbed, for he could not be idle. First one boy came, and in fourteen days the number increased to twenty-three, most of them Jews. His school became so large that he had to seek for larger quarters. Though sick, he performed a herculean task. His school grew until it had fifty children, most of them Jews. He taught them Christ. The Jews roused opposition against him and took their children away, but the children persisted in coming. And when a Jew told one of the little girls that Jesus was not God, she began to cry and accused him to her mother as an unbeliever. In 1847 he was compelled to go to Pressburg for his health, but there he preached Christ to the Jews. He returned to Pesth to undergo a terrible operation in his legs. But he bore it with patience, and from his sickbed still kept on teaching the boys, until his school had grown to 120 children. His sufferings increased, yet he said: "My body is decaying, but my inner man lives and grows." God called the sufferer home, September 27, 1849. His life had been a wonderful witness for Christ in the midst of pain. And though dead, his influence remained. The school he founded has become, forty-six years after, a large institute, and had a few years ago over five hundred pupils.

But the influence of these Jewish converts, who joined the Reformed Church of Pesth, has not yet ended. One of the sisters of Philip and Adolph Saphir married Rev. C. H. Shonberger. He, too, had been converted at Pesth and had joined the Reformed Church. He became a missionary to the Jews at Prague in 1871. One of his converts was Rev. A. Venetianer, who became a Reformed minister. And now comes the strangest coincidence, and with it we close this remarkable story of the Reformed and the Jews. A number of years ago a Jewish rabbi in southern Russia, named Rabbinowitz, became a believer in Jesus, and startled his synagogue by preaching the Gospel of "Brother Jesus." His synagogue followed him into Christianity. But who was to baptize his people with

Christian baptism? The writer remembers about the year 1884 seeing an advertisement in the Reformed Kirchenzeitung of Germany by the little Reformed congregation at Rohrbach, near Odessa, in Russia, asking for a pastor. For a time this call from this distant Reformed Church seemed to get no response. Then in the providence of God it was accepted by the Reformed pastor of Trieste, Austria, Rev. Mr. Venetianer, the convert of Schonberger. And now notice the coincidence of providence. Venetianer went there as pastor. And as he was a Jewish convert, he was called in by Rabbinowitz to baptize in his congregation, which Vanetianer began by baptizing the first convert October 2, 1887, and he wrote later that he baptized three children of Rabbinowitz. What will be the future influence of that Jewish movement in southern Russia under Rabbinowitz no one can measure, but it will be great. Here again we see the Reformed were a link to aid the Jews into the Church. And Pastor Venetianer was doing what Pastor Torok had done at Pesth many years before.

Such has been the influence of the work among the Jews at Pesth, in which the Reformed Church was active in aiding the Presbyterians. It brought very prominent Jews into the Christian Church, as the Saphirs and Edersheim. It led to the founding of a most successful and active German Reformed Church at Pesth, now numbering more than 1,500 members. It has led to a revival and strengthening of the evangelical party in the Hungarian Reformed Church until it is now in the ascendency in that Church, led by such men as Professor Balogh, of the University of Debrezin, and Professor Szabo, of the University at Buda-Pesth.

Chapter II.

FERDINAND W. BECKER.

Another witness for the Reformed Church among the Jews was Rev. Ferdinand William Becker, "a hero of Jewish work," as his biographer calls him. He was of Reformed birth, having been born in the Reformed county of Wittgenstein in Germany, March 27, 1797, and baptized by Rev. J. D. Otterbein, of the Otterbein family, famous in the Reformed Church of Germany in the Nineteenth century. His father died when he was three years old, leaving his mother with six small children. He was often, therefore, in needy circumstances and when young was put out to work at the joiner's bench and behind the counter.

In 1816 he went to Elberfeld, where under its earnest religious life he was converted, when G. D. Krummacher (the revival Boanerges of the Reformed there), and Doring of the Lutheran Church, had brought religion to a high state of activity. It was Doring's question, "Do you love Jesus?" that led to his conversion in his room September 13, 1816. He at once showed great inclination for religious work and as Doring thought he was too old to begin to study for the ministry he suggested that he become a missionary. He was introduced to the Missionary Society at Elberfeld and accepted by them June 2, 1817.

On June 20 of that year he entered the Mission House of Janicke in Berlin, remaining there for three years. Then he went to England to continue his studies. At Cambridge he came under the influence of Joseph Wolff, the famous converted Jew, and missionary, and also of the sainted Rev. Charles Simeon. He attended the newly-erected seminary for the training of missionaries to the Jews, and completed his studies. He was appointed by the London Missionary Society for the Jews a missionary to the Jews at Warsaw, Poland, where there were forty thousand Jews.

Together with a young Englishman, McCaull, he arrived there on Christmas, 1821. But in February, 1822, the Russian government forced him to leave Warsaw. He made every effort to be allowed to return, even to going to St. Petersburg to lay the matter before the Russian court. Meanwhile he returned to England and received ordination and then was permitted to return to Warsaw.

It happened that there was a small Polish Reformed congregation there, a relic of the work of John A'Lasco, the Polish Reformer, and of the time when most of Poland had been Reformed only to be destroyed by the Jesuits later. Becker and McCaull, with their two assistants, used the little Reformed church for the worship of their mission. They were very fortunate in thus finding a place of worship. He began his work with great earnestness, but met with great opposition.

It seemed impossible to gain at first any converts. But in 1828 he baptized a Jew named Rosenfeld, who became a very zealous evangelist, bringing many from the synagogue to the church. In the same year a prominent Jewish Rabbi named Schwarzenberg became a Christian and preached Christ among the Jews, often in great danger from their fanaticism. A home for Jewish converts was founded, together with a printing establishment and bookbindery connected with it, where they could support themselves and where every Saturday a conference in the German-Jewish language was held with the Jews. In 1828 two schools for Jewish children were begun. In 1830 McCaull left to take charge of a Jewish Mission in London and Becker was made superintendent of the mission at Warsaw.

During the stormy political times of 1831 and through an epidemic of cholera he safely guided the mission work. The mission work was greatly interfered with, but soon revived. In 1833 he baptized an aged Jew named Grafstein for whom the sponsor at baptism was no less a person than the prominent citizen Count Paskiewitsch.

In 1837 two very interesting conversions took place of two young men, Henry Israelski and Sigmund Hauptman, who were students at the Jewish School for Rabbis there. They were, with most of the students, unbelieving, but came to the mission for Bibles. As they found no salvation in Judaism, they threw it overboard entirely and received Christian instruction. They were soon led to see how Jesus fulfilled the Old Testament to the salvation of their souls. They then began to speak of Christianity among their fellow students in the Jewish school. The professors prepared to force them out of the school. Meanwhile their parents began to oppress them. But they were finally baptized May 19, 1837. This caused a great sensation and great suffering to them. Hauptman's parents and some of the Jewish teachers of the Rabbi's school came to the mission house.

Hauptman was compelled to go home with his mother and Israelski, with the teachers where they disputed long with them. Israelski, after being asked whether he became a Christian because of worldly inducements, and he replied, "No," was permitted to go, and went to the house of a friend of the mission. The next day, attended by some Jews and their pupils, his father came to town to the mission to claim his son. They preached Christ to the father and some of the scholars took Christian books, but the father refused to listen. The father then went to the house where the son was staying. There the son confessed to his father his Christian belief. He wanted his son to go into the street, so that he might converse with him alone. But he refused. Then he seized his son by the throat and held him so tight that the brethren were afraid the young man would be choked, but they got him loose and talked with the father. As the father was inexorable, they took the son away into another room. The father became so wild that the police had to be sent for. Israelski afterward became a Christian minister.

In 1838 Becker stated in a sermon preached in his native city of Berleburg that in sixteen years 120 Jews had been converted. On Easter Monday (1842) the mission had the great joy of seeing five Jews baptized, one of whom underwent great persecutions. He worked for his brother as a painter, but began coming to the mission, from which he could not stay away because of the hold the truth had gained on him. He determined, therefore, in February to leave his brothers' house and come to the mission. He decided to do this on a Saturday evening, when he could get away, but he was urged to wait, as the mission house was full. But the next Saturday, in spite of the watchfulness of his brother, he came to the mission house. However already in the afternoon some of his brothers came expecting to see him at the public service. As he was not there, they asked the missionaries if he was with the missionaries. The next morning his mother appeared just at the hour of the family worship of the mission house and demanded her son with the greatest vehemence. In the afternoon other members of the family appeared. On Monday a severe storm broke out. The mother, four grown up brothers and a sister appeared, forced themselves into the mission house and especially the mother demanded to speak with the son. But the son was not inclined to do so, knowing the impetuous nature of his mother. Their rage then knew no bounds. The sons, especially one that was dumb, resorted to force. The coat of the missionary was torn from top to bottom. The missionary as well as two others of the mission house, who ran to his assistance received severe blows on the breast while the women raised a terrible outcry and several persons tried to break open the door of the young man's place of concealment. The young man crept away into the room of the missionary's wife, but the Jews forced themselves to it. Finally police help having been called the tumult was stilled. This caused great excitement and other Jews came which only gave the missionaries additional opportunities to preach Christ to them. To his relatives he boldly declared, "I seek nothing but Christianity." He then confessed Christ at baptism.

On the mission house there was a window on which there were, in Hebrew, the words of Isaiah, fifty-fifth chapter, "Ho, every one that thirsteth," etc. The Jews passing by would often stop, read it, and inquire the meaning of those words on that house, then come in and allow themselves to be addressed by the missionary. Often there would be quite a gathering of them in the street before this Scripture sign whom the missionary would address.

In 1841 Becker celebrated at Elberfeld the twenty-fifth anniversary of his ordination, and also at London where he addressed various religious gatherings.

In 1855 the mission at Warsaw had to be discontinued. On December 22 all the missionaries were required to bring their official documents before the Lutheran Ministerium and it was made known to them that it was the Czar's will that they should leave. This came like a thunderclap and was the result of the Crimean war, where England had joined her forces with Turkey and France against Russia. But it was not supposed that the Jewish Mission at Warsaw, although under the English Society, would be endangered, especially as Becker was a German and not an Englishman. On February 8, 1855, Becker and West, the two missionaries, were compelled to leave Warsaw. But at the railroad station people of all classes, Protestants, Catholics, Greeks, Jews, proselytes, gathered in their honor to bid a sad farewell to them. The railroad station was so crowded that it was hardly large enough to accommodate the throng. This mission was not resumed by the Society until 1876.

Becker then proceeded to a new field of labor at

Hamburg. Here he found the work much more difficult than at Warsaw. In the French Reformed church there he began holding his services in German July 1, 1855, for Jews and Christians. He often preached in the German and English Reformed churches in Hamburg and Altona, as also in the Reformed church of the neighboring city of Lubeck. His work was much more scattered than in Poland, stretching out into the neighboring districts of Mecklenburg, etc., and he was often away from home by the week. Yet he found the field ripe for harvest. On the fiftieth anniversary of the London Society for the Jews, 1858, he returned to London, where he preached the festival sermon. In it he gives the statistics of the work in Poland. "Poland was our Palestine. More than 100 proselytes were trained in the mission institute, 5,000 Polish New Testaments and 125,000 tracts were published, and 360 persons were converted through the mission. So that his work there was not fruitless.

Later, when Rev. Mr. Harms, pastor at Hermansburg, who had founded a famous foreign mission supported by his congregation alone, attacked missions among the Jews as useless, Becker replied in a pamphlet. In it he argued strongly from Scriptures on the importance of work among the Jews. In 1856 he preached in the synagogue at Berleburg, his birthplace, on Hosea 3:4, 5. When the Jewish worship had ended he asked permission to speak. In it he claimed that this chapter had been darkened by the Rabbis because they did not refer it to a Messiah. He asked his countrymen to think over these things and to believe on Christ. Most of the men remained in the synagogue, about thirty, and many women. But opposition began to show itself there. One said that the synagogue was not the place for such exhortations. So he left the synagogue but later he heard them discussing the sermon on the streets. He took advantage of it to scatter tracts. In the afternoon of that day he found a number of Jews in the Berleburg park and spoke to them on Zechariah 3:14, and soon a dozen of them gathered around him. His address and efforts made a deep impression on some of their minds.

In April, 1862, he caught a severe cold in holding a service of the Jews in a subterranean clothes depot. He preached for the last time June 3, 1862; but, though unable to preach after that, he still labored among them as he could in his house. He said: "O if I could only each day say to some Jew, Christ stretches out his arms to him." But soon even this was forbidden on account of his health. At Christmas time his sickness greatly increased and by January 5 his sufferings became so great that he earnestly prayed the Lord not to lay his hand too heavily on him. His last day was a Sabbath. "Help, Lord, help; O come, my Saviour," he cried. His last word was "Jesus." On his tomb in the German Reformed churchyard are Romans 14:8 and Philippians 1:21, on the first of which Dilthey preached his funeral sermon.

He was a very devoted missionary to God's ancient people. For Biblical controversy he had remarkable gifts, especially on the Old Testament prophecies of Christ. He was very tactful to turn everything so that he might speak to the Jews about Christ. "Have you a new Testament," was asked a Jewish keeper of a bookstore. As he showed him a Bible he asked him if he had read the second part. He replied that he had read the Book of Revelation. Becker called his attention to the New Jerusalem of that book and then passed on to Isaiah fifty-third chapter, pointing him to Christ. "But," replied the Jew, "I will have sins again." Becker replied, "In Christ is justification and strength." Finding some young Jews talking in a park about a lottery, Becker took the part of one of them who opposed lottery. Two of them said that lotteries were necessary so as to get enough to eat and live. Becker called their attention to Matthew 6:33, "Give us this day our daily bread." He thus introduced Christianity to them and urged it upon them. To a dealer in clothing he spoke the clothing of salvation which Christ has prepared. A woman once complained of her sore eyes. "Our Messiah," he replied, "opened the eyes of the blind and is the physician for the body and soul." Thus he preached Christ, using every opportunity to win God's Israel back to Jesus.

www.ingramcontent.com/pod-product-compliance
Lightning Source LLC
Chambersburg PA
CBHW021758220426
43662CB00006B/104